# Welcome

Having enjoyed fishing for over six decades, I've essentially educated myself in mastering the art, but that doesn't mean I know it all – on the contrary, I find I learn something new every time I fish! Every trip, be it an impromptu two hours at the local fishery or a two-week fishing holiday in Thailand, brings with it another set of unique experiences and memorable episodes. While I have tried to explain the main ways of improving your catch rate in 501 Fishing Tips, I'm certain you will be rewarded with some unexpected pleasures, including new techniques, during your own journey. At the same time, expect to learn some hard lessons – many species are hugely more intelligent than they are given credit for.

And that's why I've drawn on all my experience to bring you these updated 501 tips on coarse fishing. You should utilise the relevant tips not only to outsmart those crafty fish, but also to gain an edge on your fellow anglers. You will find that the tips will essentially save you time and money, while maximising your enjoyment of the sport.

And remember, every tip is tried and tested, so go fishing and catch some beauties!

*John*

# A unique opportunity to 'go fishing' with John Wilson around the world

## John Wilson MBE will share his knowledge and expertise with you on our unique escorted trips

Whether you want to catch sharks and tiger fish in southern Afri – Nile perch in equatorial Africa – salmon and giant sturgeon North America – or fish in many other amazing locations arour the globe, we can arrange the ideal holiday for you.

We have over 42 years experience in tailor making safa to Africa and beyond – come and share our passion for a unforgettable fishing adventure.

To find out more, speak to our specialist Christine Slater wh has in-depth knowledge of all our destinations, or conta her by email: christine@tailormadeholidays.co.uk.

tailor made holidays

☎ 020 8398 7424

www.tailormadeholidays.co.uk

*Good fishing*
*John Wilson*

Angling Projects.©
Gets Kids Hooked On Fishing Not On Drugs Or Crime.®
Junior Coarse Angling. UK.©
JCA© UK
Angling Projects & JCAUK.
Wish to Thank our Friend,
Supporter & Patron John Wilson.
Contact: Les Webber. MBE.
Tel: 0118 943 1701.
& 07831 323662.
Email: lesandjudy@supanet.com
www.angling-projects.org.uk

## Freshwater tackle

## Freshwater baits

**EDITORIAL**
**Author** John Wilson

**ART & DESIGN**
**Designer** Rob Callaghan
**Repro** Linda Duong

**ADVERTISING & MARKETING**
**Advertising Manager** Adrian Major
**Marketing** Michelle Marsh

**Management**
**Bookazine Manager** Dharmesh Mistry
(020 7907 6100 dharmesh_mistry@dennis.co.uk)
**Production Director** Robin Ryan
**MD of Advertising** Julian Lloyd-Evans
**Newstrade Director** Martin Belson
**Chief Operating Officer** Brett Reynolds
**Group Finance Director** Ian Leggett
**Chief Executive** James Tye
**Chairman** Felix Dennis



The MagBook brand is a trademark of Dennis Publishing Ltd, 30 Cleveland St, London WIT 4JD. Company registered in England



**Licensing**
This product is available for international licensing. Please contact Winnie Liesenfeld for more information winnie_liesenfeld@dennis.co.uk 020 7907 6134
Printed at BGP

1

# What's OUT THERE?

These tips will give you the secrets to my success, good luck!

"We all have the same amount of time, the question, or challenge if you like, is to decide how we use it."

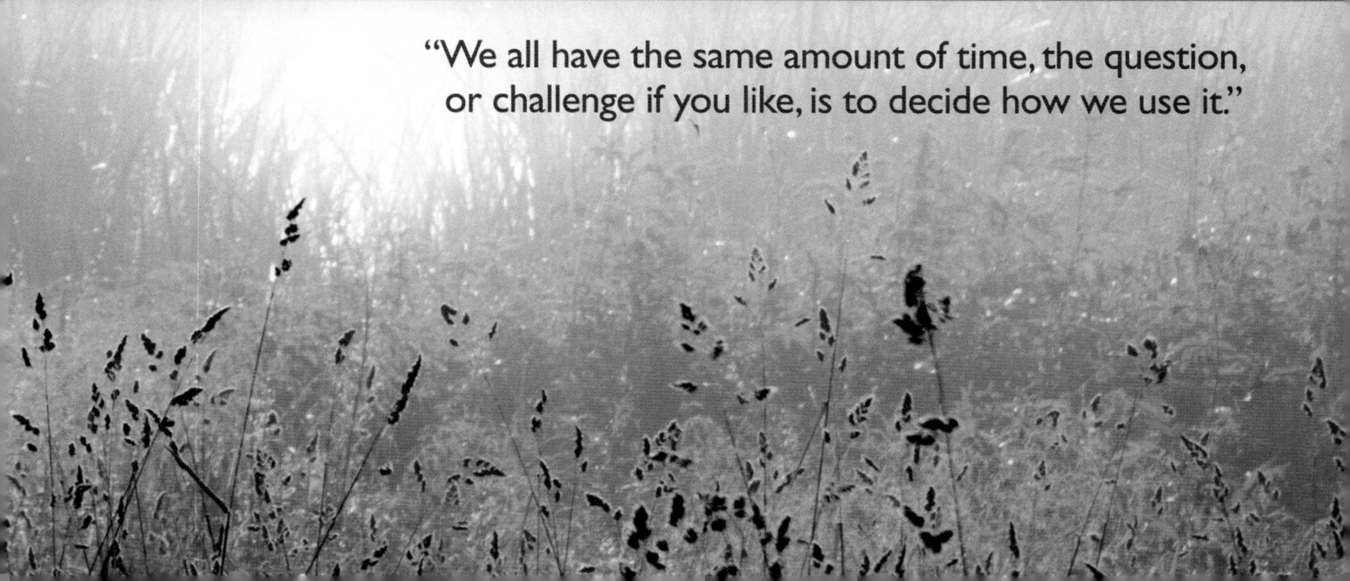

Freshwater Species

# Barbel

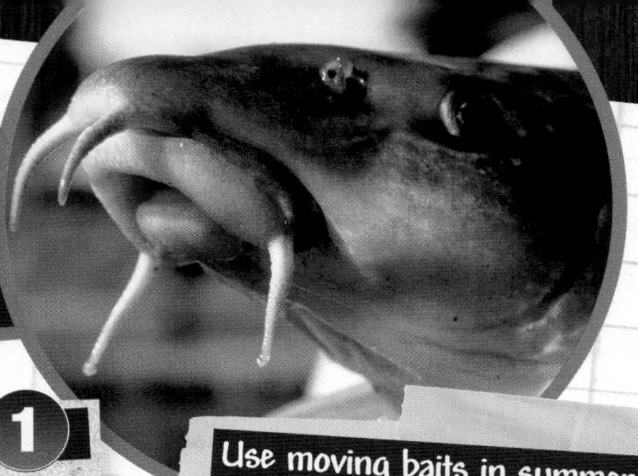

## 1 Catching barbel, avoiding chub

To stop chub from hooking themselves and disturbing the swim when barbel fishing with bolt-rig style tactics, use a 12 inch hook length and a long (1-2 inch) hair, in conjunction with a heavy 2-3 ounce running flat-bomb. Use a rubber cushioning bead between hook trace swivel and lead. They will then freely move away across the current or turn immediately downstream with the lower of your two 15-18mm boilies, large boilie or halibut pellet pursed in their lips, but usually spit it out at the last second. So only lift into a fish when the rod tip slams round and stays round, indicating a barbel has found the bait. Ignore all other pulls.

## 2 Barbel's limited visibility

Have you ever wondered why the line has a sand-papery feeling when you are touch-ledgering for barbel, or the rod tip vibrates momentarily before hooping over as a fish runs off with the bait and actually hooks itself? Well, as barbel are equipped with four long sensory barbels (hence their name), an under-slung mouth and a long snout, unlike fish such as chub, roach and tench, they actually lose visual contact with what they are about to swallow before opening their mouth. So they gently move their snout from side to side in an agitated manner, in order to centralise the bait once their mouth is open. And in so doing, their barbels must inevitably do a 'plink-plunk' against the line.

## 3 Plan and remain patient

When baiting up a swim, try loose feeding by hand from a spot several yards upstream to allow for the pace of flow to ensure the food is deposited exactly where you want it on the river bed. Alternatively, use bait droppers full of maggots, hempseed or 3-6mm pellets - possibly the three most effective attractor loose feeds for barbel. With either of the above methods, try not to fish immediately afterwards. Action is invariably more hectic and lasts for longer if you first allow the barbel to move into the swim and over the bait, gaining confidence in their feeding, for at least an hour or so, before your hook rig is presented to them.

## 4 Buy chest-high waders

To get the most out of your river, especially when exploring those barbel-holding runs beneath willows and lines of alders along the opposite bank, you need to get in with the fish, at least into the centre of the river, in order to trot a bait through steadily and directly downstream. This means investing in a pair of lightweight, chest-high, waders. The best are breathable and come with hard-wearing neoprene reinforcement at the knees and built-in neoprene socks. You then simply slip on felt-soled wading shoes for maximum stability over slippery stones and boulders. Anyone who fly fishes for salmon or sea trout, or who long trots for grayling during the winter months, will no doubt be equipped already. Either way, quality chest-high waders are a sound investment for enjoyment, allowing you to also kneel and sit down on the bank anywhere along the river without the need for a stool.

## 5 Use moving baits in summer

During the warm summer and autumnal months, barbel are far more likely to move across the flow and intercept a moving bait, even one being trotted through at current speed, than later on in the year when temperatures start to plummet. So get to enjoy catching some barbel on the float, using a powerful 13 foot trotting rod and centre-pin reel holding 6-8lbs test. Keep a selection of both heavy Avon and Chubber floats in your waistcoat, and be sure to split their bulk shotting capacity of say 3-5 swan shots, into a line of AAs fixed onto the line 12-16 inches above the hook, with a small shot or two in between. See Grayling Tip 142.

## Go fish spotting 6

If like me you welcome the rest provided by the statutory closed season for rivers, but after a few weeks start to get itchy to be beside water, why not pay your favourite barbel stretches a visit? From around the beginning of May onwards (depending upon water temperatures), barbel congregate upon the gravel shallows in readiness for spawning, and so there is no better time for fish-spotting, and ascertaining to exactly what size they grow along a particular part of the river. So don't forget the Polaroid glasses.

## Plan to fish in the dark 7

When clear-water barbel do not play ball and move up into a pre-baited swim, pushing smaller fish species out of the way, then plan to fish for them during the hours of darkness. This reluctance to feed aggressively during daylight hours is common place in stretches of river where the barbel are targeted daily, particularly with small groups of known or specimen-sized fish that have been repeatedly caught and know all the tricks. So plan to start an hour or so before dusk, expecting no small level of response once the light has totally gone, and be prepared to fish on for some while until they do respond. Those first few hours of darkness are usually best. But don't forget a trip during that first hour or two before dawn, which can so often produce, especially during the warmer months.

## Use a back lead 8

When ledgering at close range bolt-rig style for barbel (or carp) in really clear water, where they can be viewed moving all around the bait to inspect it, it pays to incorporate a back lead positioned on the line 2-4 feet above the bait. Simply and loosely pinch onto the line two 3x swan shots, or sleeve a coffin ledger onto the line and secure with a rubber sliding float stop at each end. This ensures that the line above your ledger rig is ironed flat to the river bed, thus alleviating any chance of lines bites and fish spooking through their fins touching the line. It is especially important when having to fish from high-bank swims, where the line would otherwise angle down sharply from rod tip to ledger rig.

## Bait droppers 9

For depositing any kind of loose feed straight down to the river bed of close-range swims (say up to a rod length and a half out) regardless of current force, bait droppers, which come in all shapes and sizes, are worth their weight in gold. Monster droppers holding half a pint of hempseed, maggots or pellets get the job done in no time at all and minimise disturbance, though you do need a long, stiff rod to swing a large full dropper out. And droppers must be swung out and not cast, otherwise bait could get distributed all over the place. And you want it concentrated within a relatively small area over which the barbel will eventually move and start hoovering it up. Beware of the odd pike which appear from nowhere to attack the lid of the dropper when it hangs down and flaps in the current as you lift it out.

## The luncheon meat tip 10

One of the most satisfying and pleasing techniques for catching barbel occurs during the warmer months when donning chest-high waders and getting into clear-flowing, gravel-bottomed rivers. Carefully wade out to a position immediately below a shoal of fish (which can often be seen hugging the bottom in the runs between long beds of flowing weed) and cast a chunk of luncheon meat upstream and slightly across, so it rolls back along the bottom directly in line with the shoal. And to do this you must allow an all-important bow to form in the line between rod tip and bait.

# Freshwater Species

# Barbel

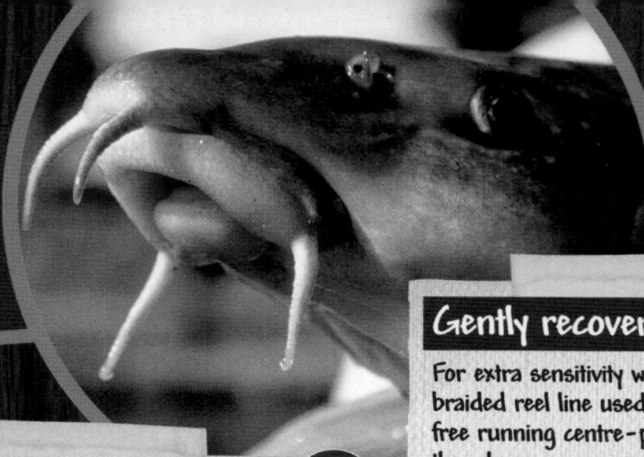

## 11 Why roll meat?

Rolling meat, as the method has been dubbed, works effectively for one main reason. The free lined bait is brought down to the shoal at current speed, like all loose particles of natural food, so their suspicion is not aroused. Moreover, it comes directly down river, tumbling along the gravel, and is not dragged unnaturally across the fish's vision, which is what the line would do if you were situated on the bank and not standing in the water immediately downriver.

## 13 Different hook weights

You can make up several different weights of hooks (to cover all conditions from slow currents to turbulent runs) simply by using different thicknesses of lead wire. Large sizes of wide-gape-eyed hooks from 6 up to 2 will serve you best. And in addition to luncheon meat, tinned ham, sausage in skins, etc, even good old bread flake and protein pastes will all make this method work and come alive.

## Gently recover line

For extra sensitivity when rolling meat, a braided reel line used in conjunction with free running centre-pin reel is hard to b though you can manage with a fixed spoo reel and monofilament. The secret is to a gently recover line as the bait is brought to you by the current, whilst keeping that in the line, which could suddenly tighten completely fall slack as a fish hoovers up bait and belts downstream towards you.

## Use scented paste

When bolt-rig style ledgering for barbel (a chub), particularly when the river is in full and visibility is at an all time low, give your added attraction by moulding a large dollop soft, aromatic paste around your hair-rigge boilie or halibut pellet. As pieces break off o pecked off by small fish and roll downstrea barbel will follow the scent up to your hook

## 12 Use lead wire

To facilitate casting, and to counteract the bait's inherent buoyancy when rolling meat so it tumbles along naturally, a slither of lead wire (roofing lead is exactly the right thickness) is super-glued to the top of the hook shank and firmly whipped over with black fly tying thread. Chamfering each end of the lead with your thumbnail makes for an extremely neat finish. See Diagram below. The hook, now looking decidedly shrimp-like with its curved back, will always present the bait with the hook point angled upwards, and is thus less likely to catch upon snags or weed. Generally, however, large chunks of meat are used in order that the hook is not actually visible.

## Extra boilies

When smaller specimens pick your ledgered size 10-15mm or pellet hook bait, simply tie longer hair to accommodate t size 20mm boilies or a 25mm halibut pellet. The mouth of a double figure barbel can easi hoover them up.

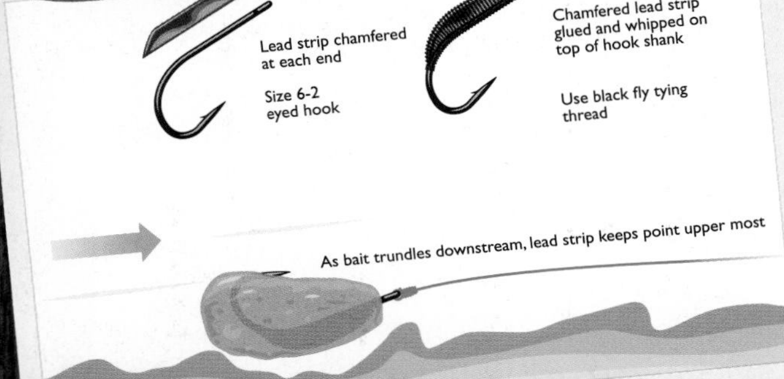


## 17 Big barbel

If you have your sights set on a really big barbel, remember that a September fish, for instance, could weigh as much as 10-15% more towards the end of the season in March. So providing the weather stays mild, concentrate your efforts during those precious last two weeks of the river season.

## Stock up on maggots 18

There's no doubt about it, barbel love maggots. Trouble is, so does every other cyprinid species, so wherever small, nuisance fish share a particular swim with barbel you must be prepared to feed them off. And that means having enough maggots to keep loose feeding until all the lesser fish are literally full up. Keep a steady stream going through the swim, either by throwing in maggots by hand or depositing them straight down to the bottom of really fast runs through continual use of a bait dropper. In small rivers a gallon of maggots is not excessive, while in rivers twice the size, you'll need twice as many maggots. But eventually, and it may take an hour or two, those barbel will be the only fish still munching maggots. Then you could clean up. And in clear-flowing swims where the fish are plainly visible, try selecting a particular specimen and watch it hoover in your bunch of maggots.

## Stret-pegging 19

If you're planning to catch barbel from a deep, even-paced run close into the bank, then why not anchor your bait to the river bed using a mini link-ledger, but have a float to watch on the surface? This devastatingly effective rig is called stret-pegging and allows you to watch a float (which must lie flat on the surface) due to the exaggerated subsurface bow in the line between float and link-ledger. You simply set the float, a Chubber, Avon or large Balsa, fixed with silicon tubing at both ends, at least twice the depth of the swim (keep pushing it up the line until the set-up works) and cast directly downstream. See Diagram below.

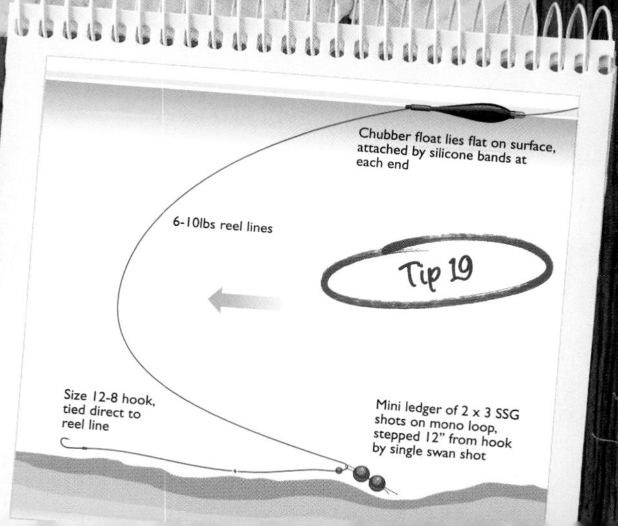


## The master technique 20

Once the mini ledger (in slow swims a single swan shot is sufficient) has anchored the bait to the bottom, the secret of stret-pegging is in allowing a little loose line for the subsurface bow to form and the float to settle lying flat, before placing the rod in two rests with the tip angled up a little. The float should now be swaying gently from side to side in the current (literally any speed water may be fished in this way so long as your float is set far enough over depth), and when a fish takes the bait, it will cock and glide positively under all in one. A lovely sight to see, not only when barbel fishing, because any bottom-feeding river fish may be caught stret-pegging. See Carp Tip 54.

## Use an Avon-style rod 21

Though float fishing, the close-in technique of stret-pegging is best executed using a 11-12 foot Avon-style rod, rather than a lighter waggler rod.

# Bream

## 22 Float ledgering

Want to catch bream on the float that are feeding over weed or amongst cabbages in still or slow-moving water? Then float ledgering is often the answer, using a peacock quill waggler float (attached with silicon tubing around the bottom end – not locked with shot) and set a foot or two over depth. Don't use a small bomb stopped several inches from the hook by a small shot because it will drag the bait and hook length into the weed and minimise bites. Far better to use a 20-30 inch (depending upon weed density and height) weight link, joined to the reel line 20-24 inches above the hook using a four-turn water knot. And simply pinch 2-3 large swan shots onto the end of the link. Don't worry about the float's actual shotting capacity.

## 24 Remain poised to strike

Rather than wait for difficult-to-miss slammers which rarely materialise when quiver-tip ledgering rivers for winter bream, be prepared to strike at any strange movement on the tip. Keep the rod angled up high (on two rests) to alleviate excess current pressure against the reel line, and you'll find that just holding bottom (and this is the secret) with two or three 3x swan shots, is possible in the strongest flow.

## 25 Drop backs

Drop-back indications are often the bites to look for when quiver-tipping for bream, whe the tip suddenly and seemingly without reas momentarily eases or jerks back because the shots have slightly mov due to a bream inhalin the bait. Forward pulls and vibratory pulses of the tip are also worth hitting, but those drop-backs will put far more bream in your net. So juggle about with the amount of shots on you ledger link, ensuring that they only just hold bottom. Anything more or less, is a bite.

## 23 Use buoyant baits

Use buoyant baits when float-ledgering, like bread flake or crust that will lie on top of the weed, and remember to angle the rod top upwards in a flow, in order to ensure that minimal line is on the surface, so as to stop the float tip from pulling under. But when your rig is settled on the bottom, you can tighten up so that only a small part of the tip is showing. Bites are registered by the float tip simply disappearing positively, though occasionally by it rising, if a bream lifts the shots from the weed. Works well for tench, and carp too.

## 26 Spotting silver bream

The silver bream is in British waters extremely rare, and mainly confined to East Anglia and the Midlands. This decidedly delicate-looking fish takes most small baits used for roach and rudd and prefers still and slow-moving wate It lacks the thick covering of mucus associated with commo bream, and the scales are quite large and noticeably silver hence its name. It has a small head, large eyes and less of a protrusible mouth than common bream. When erect, the silver bream's dorsa is unusually high, and its pector pelvic and anal fins (unlike t common bream) show a of orangey-pink, ra similar to the c

## Bulk up the shots

**27**

When slider-float fishing for bream in deep, still waters, always use a bodied-waggler float carrying more shots than would seem necessary. This is to ensure the reel line passes freely through the float's eye or ring, quickly taking the bait down to the bottom. Bulk most of the shots (against which the float will rest for casting) 3-4 feet above the bait, with two small shots in between, the lowest positioned 6-10 inches from the hook actually resting on the bottom. Using several inches of slightly finer line, tie a five-turn stop knot onto the reel line above the float at the desired depth for bait presentation, leaving both ends 1-1½ inches long, ensuring they fold when passing through the rod rings. If the float's bottom ring or eye allows the stop knot to slip through, use a tiny (2-3mm) bead between it and the knot.

## The slider-float fishing technique

**28**

Remember always to dip the rod tip immediately after casting when slider-float fishing, and wind like crazy for a few turns, in order to ensure all the line sinks between float and rod tip to counter act any sub-surface draw. Quickly open the reel's bale arm, allowing line to peel freely from the spool and eventually through the float's bottom ring until the bait touches the bottom and the float cocks. Lastly, remember to strike sideways in order to pull the line through the water and the hook into the bream, as opposed to losing striking power by trying to lift the line against surface tension, which is next to impossible!

## rporate a bolt rig into your end tackle

**29**

distance ledgering for big, still-water bream, hitting bites is always a m. Taking a leaf from the carp angler's book, however, by incorporating a shock, or bolt rig into your end tackle, will result in those bream actually a small hook into themselves. Method feeders with internal elastic are much ed (which alleviates snap-offs), to which a short 4-5 inch hook length of est soft braid is tied with a size 12 or 10 hook on the business end. As for ne, do not go below 8lbs test due to the long casting of a heavy ball of bait.

## winger-type bite indicator

**30**

e bait for distance ledgering for bream like a 10mm boilie, pellet, or three ains of corn, is hair-rigged. Immediately prior to casting, a ball of method-ix ground bait (to which hempseed, corn, casters and chopped worms, have een added) is firmly moulded around the feeder, with the hook bait carefully idden inside. After casting to the desired spot (use a marker float cast out sing another rod, so all the bait ends up within a relatively small area), the line tightened up, and a heavy, swinger-type bite indicator clipped onto the line (on short drop) in front of the bite alarm. Should a bream swim towards the rod, e indicator will fall and indicate a drop-back bite.

## Avoiding the drift

**31**

When fishing the waggler for bream in still water, one of the most common problems is avoiding the drift. So here are three tips for beating it. Start by sloshing a finger full of washing up liquid around the line on your reel's spool, which will quickly sink the line. Second, use a really long, straight peacock waggler with a bulk shot capacity of at least four to five SSG shots so all the locking shots are well beneath the surface and below the top drifting layer. And lastly, fish over depth with one or two No 6 or 8 shots dragging along the bottom, which acts like a brake to help keep the bait in position.

Freshwater Species

# Bream

## Feeder fishing & plugging 32

Feeder fishing for bream in still waters usually revolves around incorporating a clear plastic open-end or cage-type swim feeder made from wire mesh, into your ledger rig. A fixed paternoster tied using a four turn water knot is best for this. And plugging, as it is often called, is the secret to this method, because you don't want feed coming out on the cast and baiting up areas you're not fishing. Start by pressing one end of your feeder into the ground bait mix (not over-dampened), gently pressing the ground bait inside to block that end. Then put in some loose feed, sweet corn, casters, finely chopped worm etc, but leave enough room at the opposite end for another plug of ground bait. Finally, squeeze tightly at both ends using thumb and forefinger, immediately before casting, and providing you have not over-wetted the ground bait, the feeder will explode its contents ONLY when it reaches the lake bottom.

## Use a fixed paternoster 33

When standard ledgering or feeder fishing for bream in both still and running water, regardless of whether you use a swing tip, a quiver tip or a hanging bobbin-type indicator, a running ledger is not required. The simple fixed paternoster is the best rig by far, and to make one simply tie an 8-10 inch length of line (could be reel line or thicker) onto your mainline using a four-turn water knot. This forms the link to which shots, bomb or feeder are attached. For feeders and bombs, add a tiny snap swivel to facilitate quick changing. How far up the line from the hook you tie this link depends on whether you are presenting a static bait, or are hoping to encourage bites on the drop. For the latter, start with a tail of around 4-5 feet. For static baits, 18-24 inches is ideal. If you wish to use a hook tail of a lighter breaking strain than your reel line, for a more natural presentation of say slowly falling baits like casters and maggots, then simply tie this, again using the four-turn water knot 10 inches from the end of your mainline, which itself then becomes the ledger link. See diagram below.

## Swing tip

When ledgering in still and slow-moving river for bream, quiver tip and bobbin-type bite indicators are not only more commonly used th the swing tip, but they a more versatile. Though unbelievably sensitive, the trouble with swing tips is that they wobble about too much when trying to cast any reasonable distance, causing the mainline to wrap around the rod tip and tangle. Swing tips do however have one redeeming feature, and that is showing the difference between line bites and true bites. Liners cause the tip to twitch and jiggle about in short, sharp lifts, whereas with true bites the tip continues to rise until it points directly at the bream. Or, should the bream swim towards the rod, thus moving the lead or feeder, the tip simply falls back dramatically. So in certain circumstances, especially for short to medium-range ledgering, there is still good reason for using a swing-tip indicator.

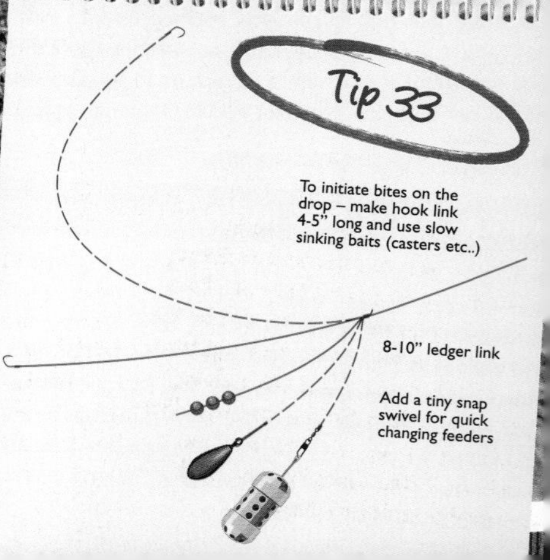

## 35 ıge feeders

en feeder fishing for bream in shallow waters, say, less than 6 foot deep, put r faith in plastic or wire mesh cage-ders. These ensure that the ground bait ng explodes quickly and easily, forming attractive cloud that doesn't spook the n. But you don't want this to happen if gering a 20 foot deep swim in Ireland's t-flowing River Shannon, where a ge, open-end, clear, plastic feeder will ain the bait as it sinks and release only h impact with the river bed. Remember. shing is horses for courses.

## 36 up your feeder mix

ou are distance-ledgering a still water it requires constant baiting with ground it balls, add a few drops of oil-based liquid ditive to your feeder mix on the next cast, leave a slick on the surface, as a target for ming your ground bait.

## 37 olaris slider float

o catch big bream on static baits that are tuated within pole range in both wide, deep vers (6-20 foot plus) and smaller, deep d fast flowing rivers, consider a Polaris der float set-up. The wire-stemmed laris slides on the 4-5lbs running line nch a small shot at mid depth against ich it rests while being shipped out) and omatically locks like magic (via the Frixon ice at the float's base) at the desired th once the one ounce bomb has settled. a four-turn water knot to attach a 12 hook link 5 inches above the bomb, and h on a tiny shot 5 inches above the hook eep the bait anchored to the river bed.

## 38 windy conditions

uiver-tip ledgering for bream in e, open waters, remember that during emely windy conditions there will be a siderable subsurface tow caused by the es hitting one end of the lake, which sequently forces surface water down, back up the lake. So for maximum line k-up on the strike, sit parallel to the nk actually facing wind direction, and ke sweeping, sideways strikes.

## 39 The Polaris setup

You never know when you might be wanting to slider-float fish for bream in excessively deep still water, so always keep a few Polaris floats in your box. Setting up these self-locking floats is easy. Thread your reel line down through one of the two holes in the tubular Frixon locking device at the bottom, and make up a fixed paternoster end rig incorporating either a bomb or feeder rig. The small hole accommodates lines in the 3-6lbs range and the larger, heavier lines. Then pinch on a No 1 shot 3 feet up the line for the float to rest against when casting. It is imperative not to use less weight in the terminal set up than is recommended, otherwise the float's buoyancy will only drag the bait along the bottom when you try to tighten up.

## 40 Use small hooks

Float ledgering using a Polaris is the best way of beating that eternal problem experienced when ledgering for bream line bites. But because of the enormous right angle of line that exists between bait and rod tip once the float has automatically locked, setting large hooks at distance can prove troublesome. So use smaller hooks and smaller baits when fishing the Polaris and, if you do inexplicably miss bites, try winding in fast for a couple of seconds before lifting the rod into a strike. This will effectively take up that slack line.

## 41 Night fishing success

Having trouble getting the specimen-sized bream of rich and clear water lakes or pits to pick up your baits during daylight hours? Then simply fish for them during darkness when they naturally feed more ravenously.

# Carp

## Use the lift method

42

One of the most simplistic and, consequently, delightful ways of catching carp (any sized carp) at close range, is fishing the lift-method. Attach 4-6 inches of peacock quill to the bottom end only with a sleeve of silicon tubing set slightly over depth (locking shots result in the line breaking should a carp plunge through weeds). Using a reel line of around 8-10lbs test, with a single swan shot pinched on 5-6 inches above a size 10-8 hook, completes the rig. Bait can be pellets, maize or small boilies, hair rigged, with loose feed of the same or smaller, pellets or particles. The permutations are like carp fishing itself - endless.

## The lift method technique

When fishing the lift, the rod is best supported (no rod rests are used for this techniq
beneath the forearm and rested upon your knee, after an underarm-flick cast is made
several feet further out than you have introduced loose-feed. This is for good reason,
because you need to quickly wind the rig back (with the float well clear of the surface) s
the exposed hook does not catch up on bottom debris, or the shot bump into feeding ca
before allowing it to settle on the bottom directly amongst the loose feed. Gently tighten
line so the float is all but cocking and wait, whilst holding the rod throughout. Line bites
will make the float sway and jerk, almost dipping it under at times, as the tails or pectoral
fins of carp momentarily catch the line - one reason why I like the float lying flat. Lift
bites will still be recognisable, however, whenever a carp lifts the single shot up, by the flo
suddenly drifting as though someone has cut the line with a pair of scissors. But most
bites will consist of the float suddenly cocking and disappearing all in one motion...lovely!

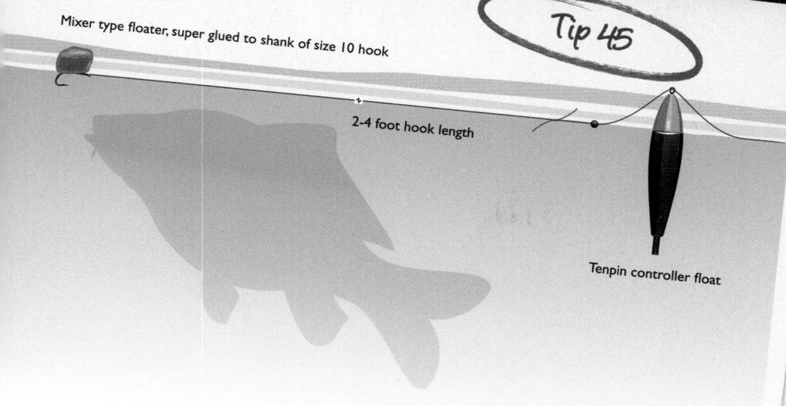


## Using small floaters 46

To present small floaters to carp like mixer biscuits, sunflower seeds, floating pellets or even small boilies etc, use a small, but strong hook (a size 10 is ideal and will land the biggest carp). To ensure it sits immediately below the floater where it is less inhibitive to a taking fish, simply cut a shallow groove in the bait using a junior hacksaw blade, and super-glue along the hook shank. Once you have mastered this technique, very rarely will a bait come off during the hardest of casts. I even glue my pellet or biscuit floaters on when fly-rodding for carp using powerful double-haul casting.

## ...arker float outfit 44

...rker-float outfit is required whenever you intend distance ...ng to an area that has been pre-baited for carp (works for ...n and bream too) using a spod or radio-controlled boat. In ...exploring with the marker float outfit is the very first task. ...an entirely separate outfit (to your fishing rods) such as a ... 12-13 foot carp or pike rod, a heavy (3-5 ounce) lead and ...-50lbs test braided reel line. Simply thread a large rubber ...d onto the end of your braided line, followed by the lead ...ich should have a large-swivelled eye) and another bead, ... tie to the bottom ring of your marker float. Be sure to use ... that incorporates a large, vane-type top that can easily be ...n at a distance. After making an exploratory cast, if your rod ...ks-up as you try to drag the lead back along the bottom, ...n you have located a weed bed. If you feel no resistance as ... lead is being wound back, then you have found a weed-free ...a, with the bottom consisting of sand, mud or silt. If, however, ...u feel a little knocking transmitted through the rod, your lead ...l be dragging over stones or a gravel bar. So select your ...hing ground and once the float is settled as a marker for ...th casting to and baiting up, sink all the line between float and ...d tip by attaching a heavy back lead close into the bank. With ...ur entire marker float line now ironed to the bottom and the ...d tip dunked below the surface and out of the way, you should ...ot catch up on it throughout the session. And it can be simply ...ound in when you leave.

## Employ latex rubber bait bands 47

Both clear and brown-coloured latex rubber bait bands, most of which come with a small, built-in dimple tab at the top through where the hook point is passed, are another excellent way of quickly attaching square-shaped floaters to your hook. Being tough and flexible, they come in varying sizes to accommodate virtually any sized floater.

## Tackling lily-bed carp 48

At some time or another everyone is faced with the difficult task of extracting hooked carp out of lilies. The secret is to watch carefully where your line actually goes into the pads, because you need to get the rod tip down low for some side-strain hauling, following the exact angle at which the carp is heading. Continue pulling with the rod nicely bent in that direction until it is hauled back, changing direction accordingly with your angle of pull each time the carp moves position. It is a strange but very effective technique. Obviously you need an all-through action rod that bends in harmony with the stretch in your line for this. It's simply no good heaving away with the rod held straight up high and fully bent if the fish has gone straight into the lilies and turned sharp right, winding the line at an acute angle around a clump of stems. The torque upon your tackle is immense. But steady and continual pressure from the right angle will surprisingly extract the largest of fish. This is one reason why I endeavour only to float fish or free line when tackling lily-bed carp. The less on the line in the way of rigs, leads, tubing, anti-tangle this and anti-tangle that, the better. And as my float (a few inches of peacock quill) is always attached with a sleeve of silicon tubing, it immediately comes off as a fish enters the pads, as does the large single shot lightly pinched onto the line several inches from the hook.

## ...witching set-ups quickly 45

...you love catching carp off the top using small floating baits like mixer biscuits and ...ating pellets, here's a useful tip that allows you to quickly change from a floating ...ntroller set-up (geared to fishing distances of up to 50 yards), to just the plain hook, for ...ose times when fish move in ridiculously close, and you merely wish to suspend the floater ...rectly below the rod tip, free-line style. Start by threading a floating controller such as a ...npin onto your 8-12lbs reel line, followed by a 3mm, black, rubber bead. Then tie a five-...rn stop knot (using a few inches of reel line) before tying on a size 10 hook direct to the ...l line 2-4 feet below the Tenpin. See diagram above. To quickly de-rig, simply work the ...bber bead over the stop knot and all the way along the hook's shank and off the point, ...lowed by the swivel at the top of the Tenpin. This literally takes seconds, and you are left ...h the bare hook. Repeat to be fishing with the controller again. Obviously, this can only ... achieved when using a small rubber bead. See Rudd Tip 228 for fishing lighter.

Freshwater Species

# Carp

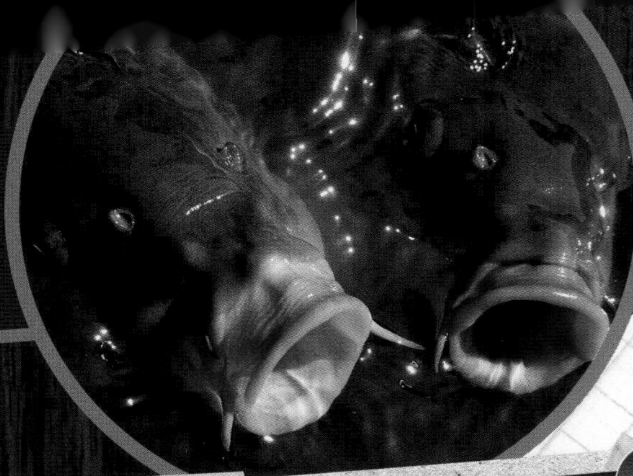

## Back leads 49

Whether ledgering for carp at close or long range, due to varying bottom contours over which your line is bound to hang, line bites can at times prove a real problem, making the carp even more wary as they approach your bait. To alleviate this, simply clip a back lead to your line immediately in front of the rod tip after casting and let it slide down to the bottom, thus pinning the line down between ledger rig and rod. Remember, however, that this only works when employing bolt-rig tactics, where due to the weight of the lead, the fish more or less hooks itself.

## Stalking belts 50

For stalking summer carp, when carrying the very minimum of tackle invariably results in more fish on the bank simply because you haven't scared the fish away from the margins, it's worth investing in a stalking belt. Designed to be worn around the waist with a variety of pockets at the side and at the rear, these bum-bag type belts are capable of holding scales, a compact camera, baits, hooks, floats, shot and rig bits etc. This leaves you free you free, clutching just rod and net, to crawl stealthily through dense vegetation in order to creep up on the whoppers slurping amongst the tree roots.

## The zig-rig 51

When the carp inhabiting large sheets of deep still water are cruising in the warm upper layers, sometimes topping, sometimes a few feet below, one technique that can really sort them out is the Zig-rig. A size 8 hook is used to present a small, rectangular, hair-rigged piece of buoyant cork, about the size of a mixer biscuit at any depth from the surface to several feet down. It resembles a pop-up boilie or imitation floater like a mixer biscuit, and is, believe it or not, readily taken. The rig comprises of a heavy in-line, semi-fixed 3-4 ounce lead, through which the mainline passes before it is attached, via the swivel, to hook a length anything up to 12 feet long. Since you are fishing deep water, this means the imitation, buoyant cork bait can be presented two feet below the surface (by far the best taking distance) in a maximum of 14 foot of water. After casting, putting the rod in its rest and tightening up, hang a weighted swinger-type bobbin on the line and be ready for strange, drop-back bites, which sometimes just keep dropping. But do not strike yet. Wait for the fish to pull the indicator up tight before setting the hook. A most versatile variation to this set up is to use a 3-4 ounce running lead with a rubber cushioning bead between lead and a buoyant, plastic sub-float. To the opposite end of the sub-float tie on a two foot hook length and hair-rigged cork bait. Once the lead settles on the bottom, free line is slowly given until the sub-float and floating bait pop up to the surface. Now slowly wind till the sub-float disappears, adding just four feet of line to the reel, if you wish the cork to be presented two feet below the surface. But it can of course be fished at any depth from two feet above bottom upwards, all the way to the surface. And there are days when it pays to experiment. So clip on an indicator and set the bite alarm. If bites do not materialise, slowly wind the sub-float and bait down to four, six or eight feet below the surface until a taking depth is found. Most fish will hook themselves whilst moving off against the buoyancy of the sub-float, and give screaming runs.

Tip 51

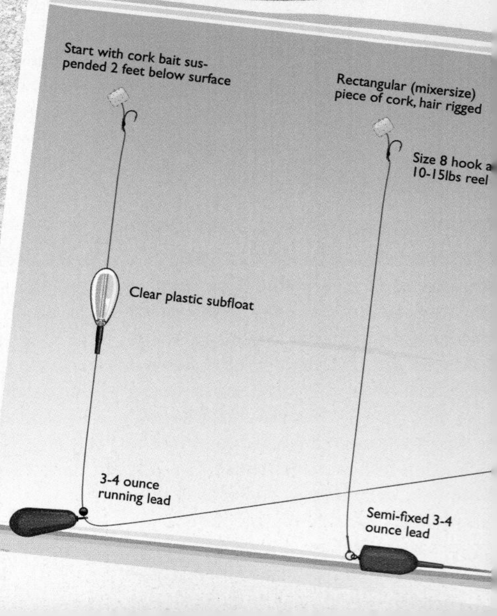

## Presenting bait in dense weed beds 52

Here's a handy tip for presenting your bait using a bolt-rig set-up to carp amongst dense weed beds when you have no option. Firstly step up your reel line breaking strain accordingly, and match it to a powerful all-through action rod, which collapses into a full bend and absorbs all the lunges of a big carp thrashing and crashing through weed beds. For the best presentation of your rig and bait, everything needs to be tucked away carefully into a clear PVA bag including a 2-3 ounce lead (to get you easily through the weed), plus some loose feed like small pellets (secure the top of the bag using PVA string or tape, so that after casting through the weed and the bag dissolves, both hook bait and freebies are in plain view and nothing is hung-up). Lastly, don't go far from your rod. It actually needs to be to hand, so that you can respond immediately to a bite by bending into a fish and hauling it around before it travels too far.

## Korda maggot clips 53

Contrary to popular belief, fuelled by the hype of pre-made bait manufacturers, plain old maggots are one of the most effective of all baits to catch carp. Trouble is, when used in ones, twos and threes, maggots are not SELECTIVE, and just about every fish in every water, from a two inch roach upwards, love them. The answer therefore is to present a real mouthful if you only want to catch larger species like carp. And a method devised exactly to this end is the Korda maggot clip. This is a cunning device that permits dozens of maggots to be threaded onto a fine wire ring without bursting any of them, which in turn is then attached (via a quick-change clip) to the loop of a hair-rig. You can even add slithers of rig foam cut to the shape and size of maggots should you wish to present your bunch of maggots pop-up style above bottom weed. Clever, isn't it?

## Stret-pegging for carp 54

With more and more carp these days making their way into British river systems from adjacent gravel pit fisheries during flood time, including some whoppers, do you fancy catching them on the float in running water? Well, then the technique of stret-pegging is simply unbeatable. And you don't need heavy tackle either. Stret-pegging in rivers is a close-range method, so a heavy Avon-style rod coupled to a centre pin or fixed-spool reel holding 8-10lbs test monofilament is quite adequate. Fix an 8-10 inch straight waggler float, or unpainted length of peacock quill onto the reel line several feet deeper than the swim (with a band of silicone tubing at each end). Ten to 12 inches above your hook (all baits and hair-rig options are open here), pinch on a single SSG shot, and above this fold a short length of mono (could be reel line) and secure as a running ledger by securing with two or three 3X SSG shots, leaving enough gap so the mini-ledger can slide up the line. Now, cast the rig directly downstream over your baited area, and once the rig has touched bottom, allow a little slack for the float to come around and lay flat. If it doesn't, push it further up the line until it does. Angle the rod on two rests with the tip pointing upwards and wait for events. From swaying gently in the current, the float will suddenly cock and slide under, all in one glorious moment. See diagram in Barbel Tip 19.

# Carp

## Dead carp 55

Should you witness the sad sight of a freshly killed, partly eaten carp lying up on the bank or in the margins of your local fishery (see photo, below), then inform the owner immediately. Such devastation is caused by otters released into a river environment where, due to cormorant predation upon silver shoal fishes combined with a much reduced annual run of eels, they roam far and wide (up to 10 miles from their home) to enjoy the easy pickings of carp stocked into still water lakes and pits, because the rivers are bare.

## Be organised 58

For targeting carp off the top when a fair amount of loose-fed floaters will get used during a lengthy session, invest in a bucket-organiser. Mine has two strips of Velcro around the sides to which an organiser wallet is quickly fixed. This holds spare hooks, floating controllers, hair needles, mini hacksaw blades, super-glue and scissors etc, while the bucket itself contains several pints of mixers or floating pellets, plus catapult, and a few tubs of alternative hook baits.

## Telescopic poles 5

When stalking for carp arou really overgrown lakes and p or rivers, don't put pressure u yourself by carting around th typical session-type landing n comprising of a short pole and large, 42-45 inch arm, triang net. Not only will it get easily tangled up whilst creeping abo but beaten carp cannot always hauled in close enough. A stron telescopic pole, however, allows you to net fish that cannot be hauled close in through weed or lilies for a big net. And with a lightweight 24-30 inch round o spoon-shaped (deep-mesh) net o the end, you can capture fish of up to at least 40lbs when they lay beaten beyond the snags and marginal screen.

## Not so cute killers 56

Contrary to popular belief, whilst otters may be perceived by the public as cute and cuddly, they are in fact indiscriminate killers. During the warmer months, they feed on frogs, toads and the spawn of both, plus newts and the eggs and young of moorhens and mallards (they also take the adult birds incidentally). When pickings are scarce in the winter, they maul or actually kill (though they never consume the entire carcass) specimen-sized carp weighing far heavier than themselves. Otters have in fact been responsible for killing carp to over 40lbs up and down the country.

## Hide the hair stop

59

When hair-rigging with particles, pellets or boilies, remember to press the Dumbell-type, hard plastic hair stop completely into the bait (by using your thumb nail) so that it is hidden. With hard pellets, simply scrape out a depression with the end of your hair needle. Carp (and barbel) have been purposefully equipped with four ultra-sensitive barbels, which have minute sensory taste-pads on the end, in order to probe through gravel, sand and into deep silt to locate small, soft items of natural food. And if a carp can locate items such as midge larva bloodworms by feeling them with its barbel-tips, it is quite capable of reacting to hard, alien objects like a hair stop, and possibly refusing your bait as a result.

## Essential attire

60

There is a clear case for wearing shorts and a pair of old shoes or trainers when stalking summer carp amongst lilies and from amongst the branches of partly submerged trees. You can then quickly get in there to apply pressure from a different angle or to untangle a snagged fish, which you might otherwise lose, without second thought.

## Prepare eyed hooks

61

To suit all your carping (tench and barbel) rig requirements during the summer ahead, tie up a selection of eyed hooks of varying sizes, each with varying length hairs to accommodate a number of bait combinations. Use a soft Dacron or braid for the hair and, after forming the loop using an overhand knot, tie on using my spade-end barrel knot (see Hooks and Rigs Tip 429). Add a spot of super-glue beneath the whipping so they do not slide up and down the hook shank.

# Crucian Carp & Grass Carp

## 62 A rare find

With massive introductions of king carp and carp hybrids to a large proportion of still water fisheries in the UK during the last 20 years, particularly commercial fisheries as they are known, finding waters containing true crucian carp is now exceedingly difficult.

## 63 Record breakers?

Most 'thought to be' record crucian carp submitted to the British Record Fish Committee, are in fact found on close inspection to be either crucian/king carp crosses (paler, slimmer fish than true crucians with tiny barbels, sometimes referred to as F1 carp) or brown gold fish/king carp or crucian crosses.

## 64 Real crucians

True crucian carp do not have barbels and rarely exceed 5lbs in weight. But they do have a slightly upturned mouth, are extremely deep-bodied, with rounded fins (which are an even, warm, grey-brown colour) and are distinctly buttery-bronze in colour with flat-lying scales. If the fish you catch do not conform to all these characteristics, then consider them not to be true crucian carp.

## 65 Lift method

As crucian carp need to almost stand on their heads (just like a tench) to inhale a bottom fished bait such as sweet corn or bread flake, pinching on a small shot somewhere (it pays to experiment until bites become positive) between one and two inches from the hook, and to strike when the float tip lifts momentarily. The way to catch the often shy-biting crucian is a scaled-down lift-float rig as used for tench, using a smaller float, less shots and smaller hooks. Bites do not always take the float under.

## 66 ecognising grass carp

king very much like a chub in the water (see Chub Tip 7), grass carp are immediately told apart by their low-set es and dark grey anal fin. They characteristically hover fferently too, just beneath the surface on warm days with heir head slightly upwards. And most importantly, in so far s the angler is concerned, they have a much smaller mouth.

## 67 eing patient

rass carp do not aggressively ngulf their food like a chub. When een sucking in small floaters from ne surface they make a point of lways pursing the bait momentarily between their lips, before sucking it back a second later. So never be in too much of a hurry to strike. If through clear water you can observe your bait in the fish's lips, always wait until it totally disappears.

## 68 For fisheries

Here's a tip for fishery owners. Grass carp are the perfect fish for stocking into British waters, because they cannot reproduce in our temperate climate. So what you stock is exactly what you end up with (less predatory losses). They will therefore not hybridise with other carps or ever over-run a fishery. Moreover, because they feed on vast quantities of soft plant tissue and do not compete directly with king carp, both can reach specimen sizes in the same fishery. What could be better?

## 69 Ideal temperatures

Originating from lowland rivers in China such as the Amur, the fertilised eggs of grass carp need to float along the surface of running water at a temperature in excess of 65F for many miles to stand any chance of hatching. This is hardly likely in the UK.

## 70 Punched bread

Though fishing punched bread is normally thought of as a winter technique for clear water canals, during the summer months it is deadly for the shy biting crucian carp. Use a 13 foot light, fine-tipped stick float rod, dot the float tip right down, and using size 18-14 hooks, nick on small pieces of fresh white bread, removed from a medium slice with a bread punch head of the appropriate size (most punches come with four or five different diameter screw-on heads). To complement punched bread on the hook, loose feed with liquidised bread on the 'little and often' basis.

Freshwater Species

# Crucian Carp & Grass Carp

## Light float rigs 71

Vastly more effective than rod fishing, is to pole fish using a light float rig to create a slow, natural fall of the bread during those last few inches above bottom. Shot the float right down to the merest 'blimp' so you can pull into the slightest sign of a bite.

## Use buoyant baits 74

When grass carp can be seen just beneath the surface but cannot be tempted to suck in a floater from the surface film, present a buoyant bait such as a pop-up boilie or floating pellet, bread crust even, (don't use anything larger than size 8-10 hooks) suspended between one and two feet below the surface. A scaled-down Zig-rig (see Carp Tip 51) is perfect for this situation. Use a two-rod set-up and try altering depths at which each bait is suspended, by recasting every half hour or so until a bite materialises.

## Know your big fish 72

Next to catfish and pike, grass carp are, pound for pound, the UK's longest freshwater species. How long will a 20lbs fish be? Possibly over three feet in length. Anything over 40lbs could measure 4 feet plus. Monsters of over 5 feet and weighing over 100lbs have been recorded in Europe, Africa and Asia.

## Playtime! 73

Be most careful when handling grass carp out of the water. They are renowned for continually jumping and flapping about on the bank, often with more vigour than during the fight. So play each one till it is exhausted before heaving out and then cover securely with the wet mesh of your net until the hook has been removed.

## Use a whip 75

Where the crucian carp of small, pea-green ponds and commercial fisheries average on the small side (up to a pound in weight), it's great fun catching them in real close. Use just the top three or four joints of a lightweight pole or Whip, with a running line of say 2lbs test tied directly to the Whip's end ring. Their dogged fighting capabilities are more appreciated without pole elastic to suppress and cushion their runs, and will give your forearm a good workout. Use an ultra-light float rig and shoot the bristle tip down to a mere whisker in the surface film before accurately plummeting depth immediately below the tip of the Whip. Feed in maggots on the 'little and often' basis (half a dozen around the float with every cast) after first introducing a few maggot-laced balls of cereal ground bait to concentrate a shoal of fish, and present a single maggot on a size 18 to 22 to a 1lbs test hook length, exactly half an inch above the bottom.

## Trophy shots 76

Take a trophy photo of your big grass carp immediately after unhooking when it is at its most knackered. Hold it horizontally between your two hands, its head towards you not the water, upside down, yes upside down (which immobilises most fish incidentally). Only turn it the right way up once you are in position, a second before the shutter is released. Don't be tempted to let it recover in a sack or tube, or you'll never be able to hold it still long enough for a photo.

## Try a caster 77

Adding a single caster to your maggot hook bait often makes crucians hang-on that much longer. Half a red worm is also worth trying.

## Don't ledger 78

At all costs do not try and catch crucian carp by ledgering. Due to their gentle feeding routine and sensitivity to resistance, you'll not even see most of the bites, let alone hit them, regardless of what indicator is used.

## Telling Crucian carp from King carp 79

Crucian carp, when feeding from the bottom, can be told apart from King carp varieties even when they cannot be seen simply by observing their feeding bubbles. Those of even quite sizeable crucians for instance, rise gently to the surface in small clusters of just 4-6 bubbles tightly grouped together. They do not burst, while those of the King carp (that are much larger) can be seen to burst after literally erupting in the surface film.

## Great baits: sweetcorn 80

If you are uncertain about baits when tackling new crucian water, float fish corn with one large kernel on a size 14 hook, after adding the juices from the tin to some brown breadcrumbs to make a ground bait. Add a handful of squashed corn kernels to the mix and feed on the 'little yet often' principle, keeping in mind that crucians are small carp.

## Catching larger crucians 81

Big, old specimen-sized crucian carp of 2lbs and upwards can become extremely cagey if regularly fished for. The secret to catching them is to fish into darkness and well into the night, using the lift-method (see Tip 65) with a luminous chemical element sleeved onto a length of slim peacock quill attached bottom end only. Hold your rod throughout, ready to strike instantly as the float keels over flat. Some bites, however, will simply take the float under, sometimes quite fast, as the crucian characteristically runs along the bottom with your bait. Bread flake, corn or worm are great after-dark offerings for big crucians.

# Freshwater Species

# Catfish

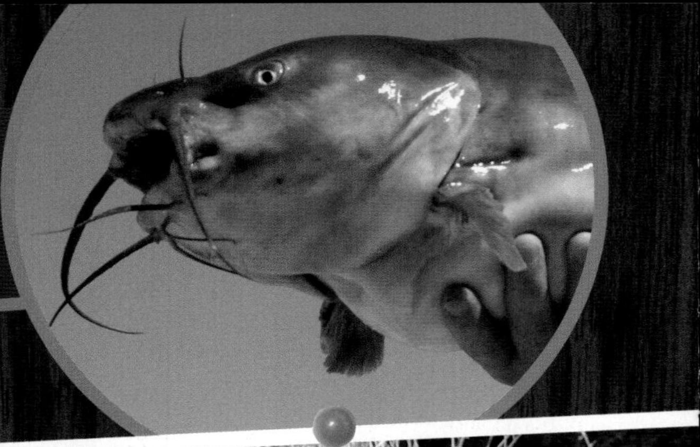

## Hola catfish! 82

For those wishing to land 100lbs-plus Wels catfish, the junction where the River Segre joins the mighty River Ebro in the town of Mequinenza in North Eastern Spain is unrivalled. A two-hour flight from Luton to Barcelona, followed by a two-hour westerly drive from the airport to Mequinenza gets you there. Contact CatMaster Tours (www.catmastertours.com; email Kate@catmastertours.com) or The Bavarian Guiding Service (www.spanish-catfish-ebro.com; email mike@spanish-catfish-ebro.com) for details.

## Bite-alarm platforms 83

For impromptu catfish sessions if the banks are nicely flat to the water, or if the swim is too difficult for bank sticks, then make your own bite alarm platform (see photo). Simply drill and glue the top two inches (hacksaw them off) from a couple of old bank sticks into a 12" x 4" x 3/4" thick piece of ply or softwood. Place eight inches apart, and screw in a couple of bite alarms. Should you require rear rests, then add rod rest tops (an inch or two higher) to another wooden platform. These take up far less room in your tackle bag than a collapsible rod-pod.

## Up for a fight? 84

Want to catch the hardest fighting freshwater species on this planet? Then the legendary Mekong catfish, which has been netted to over 600lbs but is thought to reach weights in excess of 1000lbs, is the adversary awaiting you in Thailand. Specimens up to 200lbs are purposefully stocked into many of Thailand's commercial still-water fisheries, where they have been weaned onto and are readily catchable on simple baits like bread. The most prolific of Thailand's Mekong fisheries is famous Bung Sam Ran near Bangkok. For guiding details contact: info@kiwifishingbangkok.com.

## Use fresh blood 85

Whether fishing at home or abroad for tropical freshwater catfish, all catfish (including Wels catfish) quickly home in on the blood content of baits, whether freshly killed meat, fish or fowl. Chicken heads for instance (yes beak and all, catfish don't worry about the bird's head when sucking down a duckling or moorhen from the surface) and their livers make fine baits. As do the heads of freshly killed pigeon, partridge and pheasant. All plucked of course. Simply present by hooking once only through the gristle using a size 3/0-6/0 hook (depending upon the size of catfish expected) and either ledger or free line. If you have a buddy who shoots regularly, or you shoot yourself, a supply of plucked heads can be frozen away during the shooting season which ends in February, for use throughout the summer months.

## 87 Catfishing in the UK

To find out where you can fish for Wels catfish within the UK, contact the Catfish Conservation Group, who not only control cat fisheries for their members, they list all still waters in the UK that contain the species. Their website is: www.catfishconservationgroup.com.

## 88 Visit your butcher

Offal, readily available from your local butcher, makes fine and exceptionally cheap bait for catfish. An ox heart for instance (which is getting on for the size of a rugby ball) will separate down into between 8-12 blood-filled chunks, while a pig's heart makes two great offerings. And of course the kidneys and liver of both animals are prime pussy-food. Though significantly smaller, sheep's offal works well too.

## 86 ...or eels, trout and tench

Other hot catfish baits include live and freshly killed eels, trout and small tench, with chunks of mackerel or squid topping the endless possibilities of sea baits. And when used together with a pre-baiting plan, of regularly loose feeding halibut pellets into British still-water fisheries, the same large 20-30mm sized pellets presented anywhere from two to six up on a long hair rig have proved to be one of the most effective catfish baits of all (use a daisy-chain when offering several pellets, to deter carp from getting hooked).

Freshwater Species

# Catfish

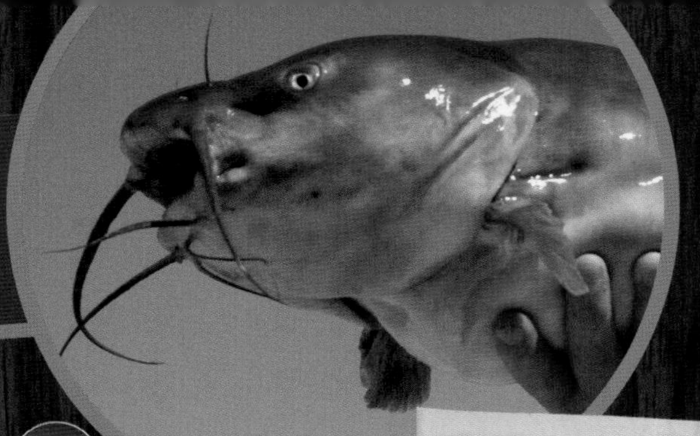

## Trot down live baits 89

Whilst there is little point in trotting down live baits in British river systems to catch catfish, because stocking them into running water is illegal, throughout Europe, particularly certain Spanish rivers (The Ebro, The Segre and The Sinca) trotting is a deadly technique because it covers so much water. Use a large 'through the middle' catfish float stopped 3-5 feet above the hook trace with a bead and power-gum stop knot. Use a strong, size 6/0, wide-gape hook on the two foot 150lbs test trace, joined to an 80lbs braided reel line by a strong swivel, with a barrel lead immediately above. An ideal live-baiting pattern, and all-round catfishing hook is the Eagle Wave big game, whose unique shape in the middle of the bend allows the bait maximum movement and good penetration on the strike. Top trotting baits are eels and small carp.

## Add a rattle 90

Want to make your live bait even more attractive? We how about adding a designer rattle to your trace, two three inches above the hook? These come in coloure plastic (white, red or yellow) and are fixed to the hook trace by laying the line in the hinge groove and snapping shut with ball bearing inside. A rubber floa stop sleeved on either side will prevent the rattle slidi These incidentally have proved effective for pike, perc and for sea species.

## Catch bigger 91

To ensure your live bait stays on the hook, and this applies particularly to barb-less hooks, simply sleeve onto the hook after the bait, a designer 'Bait Shield'. Made from thick rubber, these unobtrusive discs, available from 'Catfish Pro' are also handy when using baits on a hair such as pre-drilled halibut pellets or soft baits like liver or squid, when normal boilie-type stops are simply too small.

## Buy squid in bulk 9

By purchasing baby squid (calamari) in bulk, say several boxes at a time, from your local fishmonger or tackle specialist, there is no more economical way of ensuring that you have enough suitable bait for both hook baits and loose feeding throughout the summer months.

## The Dumbell rig 93

Presenting 5-8 inch live baits (rudd work well) just beneath the surface, especially during the hours of darkness (using th Dumbell rig) is one of the most effective ways of catching Wels catfish. As can be seen from the Diagram, after sleeving a 3-4 ounce lead onto your reel line followed by a large rubber bead, the line is threaded through a Dumbell Float and a small but strong swivel is tied on. Presentation is improved if the swivel pushes firmly into the end of the Dumbell Float, thus making it semi-fixed. Lastly, add several inches of Catlink braided trace material of 50-70lbs test and tie on a 2-3/0 hook, making sure the hook trace is slightly shorter than the length of the float. This is so that the lead touches bottom after casting and, when you tighten up to the float rig (lying flat on the surface), it is impossible for the bait to swim around the reel line and tangle. This is the beauty of this particular set-up. Always use in conjunction with an electric bite alarm and indicator, as you may not always hear that glorious smack of a catfish engulfing your bait on the surface. This technique can be most effectively used with Tip 101.

## he photo 94

r retaining catfish to photograph, e a long (6 foot x 18 inch diameter) nnel or tube made from soft, black aterial, which opens at both ends th toggles for tethering to bank cks and tension to keep straight. here really big fish are concerned, 100lbs and larger, use a stringer de from soft, nylon cord. See shwater Tackle and Lines Tips 7 and 408, for correct tying of nger loop that cannot tighten ing the time a catfish, or other e fish such as a mahseer or Nile ch, is retained.

## Chain-mail gloves 95

For bringing big catfish into the boat when fishing abroad, especially in fast-flowing rivers where landing nets are impracticable, wear a protective gripping or chain-mail glove on each hand. Then, with a firm two-handed grip of the fish's lower lip, haul it over the side using the impetus of its own body movements to your advantage.

## Catfish with only 2 barbels 96

If you catch a Wels catfish with just two small barbels under its chin, instead of the normal four, you may not have caught a Wels, but an Aristotle's catfish (Silurus aristotelis). This originates from the Akheloos River in Greece, and may have found its way into British still waters (like so many alien species) through the ornamental pond-fish trade.

## e-bait with halibut pellets 97

ou are limited in fishing hours or attempting to catch catfish m waters low in stock density, then pre-baiting can prove answer to success. Introduce, say, every other evening, erous helpings of pelleted food such as halibut pellets (which ak down and reduce to dust after 6-12 hours of being in water) or moggi chunks (which come in both halibut pellet d fish-meal flavours, and break down somewhere between -48 hours).

## Keep well back 98

Remember to set your rods well back from the water's edge, and to be particularly quiet whilst fishing at night, as catfish love to hunt really close into the margins. So position one bait no more than a few yards out.

## Watercraft 99

Watercraft plays an important part of targeting catfish during daylight hours. They love to lie under in the relative darkness and greatly reduced-light of large, overhanging trees, sunken bushes and patches of lilies.

## Essentials 100

Fish care is so important when handling catfish. A giant unhooking matt is recommended, as is a large, triangular landing net with 48-50 inch arms.

Tip 93

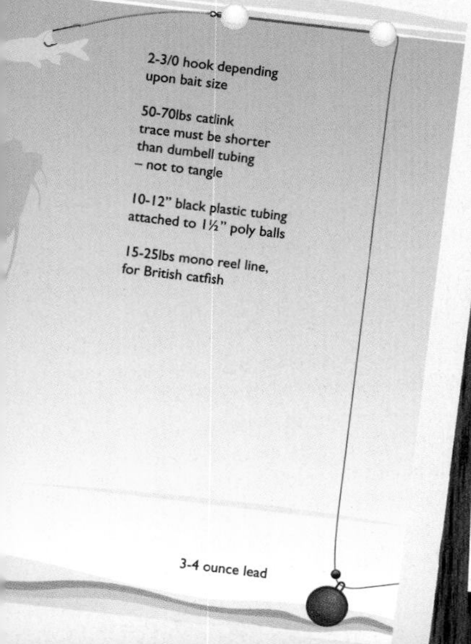


## Present distant baits by winching 101

To present both live and dead baits at distances far greater than can be cast (say 20 yards and beyond), try the unique winching method, which allows you to wind or winch your bait out to wherever you wish. Start by making up a simple end rig on your 15lbs test reel line, comprising of a 3-4 ounce bomb to which a link clip and 1/4 inch diameter curtain ring have been added, running above a snap-link swivel, with a large rubber bead in between. But don't attach your hook trace and bait just yet. And here's the clever part: have an extra rod (butt end only) ready, propped up with the butt ring facing the lake, the reel filled with just 4lbs test line, the bale arm open, and tie the end securely to the snap link on your main outfit. Now cast out the heavy lead to where you intend fishing so that both lines go out over the lake. Once your lead has settled, place the catfish rod in two rests ready for action and open the reel's bale arm, so you can wind your snap link back using the half-rod, your 15lbs main line flowing freely through the curtain ring on the lead. Once the snap link has been retrieved, simply clip on your trace and bait and wind slowly back to the lead. And hey presto, your bait is now presented way out into the lake.

CatMaster
Tours
with
Colin Bunn
and the Team
We give you more hours fishing than any other Guiding Service, the best price and No Hidden Charges
Guided Catfish Holidays
Matt Hayes
• Luxury Apartments
• All Tackle Supplied
• Fishing Licences
• Professional Guides
• Bankside Food Delivery
• Boats, Baits, Etc.
• Free Airport Pick-up
As featured on
Discovery real time
five
FOR THE BIGGEST CATFISH ON THE EBRO
Guaranteed to Catch - Make the right choice
RING FOR DETAILS, BROCHURE AND DVD
Tel: (0044) 0121 451 1861
www.catmastertours.com
Booking Enquiries: kate@catmastertours.com
CatMaster
Tours

# When the wind's in the east, the chub bite least

That old saying about an east wind is so very true, especially if you happen to live in East Anglia. Even the 'super-co-operative' chub reduces its usually aggressive bites to mere trembles of the quiver tip when a chilling east wind, straight off the sea, blows upstream along my local rivers, Wensum and Waveney. To call it a 'kiss of death' is putting it mildly. But, you know, I always take heart from the fact those chub haven't jumped out onto the bank. They are still in the river, occupying their favourite haunts. They just don't feed anywhere near as ravenously when temperatures are bordering on sub-zero.

Such conditions dictate that much consideration should be given to current patterns in each swim. For instance, areas where vortices spew up from the bottom and where the flow direction is continually changing will not house chub. Chub are not ones for moving about much in low temperatures. So it pays to study each lie for several minutes before introducing a few golfball-size lumps of mashed bread into the head of the swim, so that (taking current speed and depth into account) it eventually comes to rest on the bottom, in steady water.

Get this fundamental principle right and, whatever the temperature, bites will eventually materialise. Baiting with a fingernail-size lump of fresh, white bread flake, squeezed onto a size 10 hook on a 12-inch hook link (the shots sufficient to just hold bottom on a fixed link tied to the 5-6lbs reel line using a four-turn water knot), I'll usually wait 20 minutes or so each cast before recasting. To maximise on striking potential of what is likely to be mere one- to two-inch movements on the tip, I angle the quiver tip rod at 45 degrees to the bank. Position it straight out and you'll miss a large proportion of bites, simply because of not enough line being picked up on the strike.

Bites that many miss, and they may seem innocuous, are those sudden juddery drop backs, where the quiver tip springs back for a moment because the shots have been dislodged (the chub has the bait in its mouth at this point) before resettling into a gentle curve created by the flow. Such indications are taken, by many, as simply the movement caused by shots resettling on the bottom. But we experienced chub enthusiasts know better.

# Chub

## Learn to slow walk 102

Learn to walk slowly, when stalking chub, as though you are creeping up on rabbits in a field, picking up each foot individually. Chub, particularly big, educated specimens, are by far the spookiest to bank side vibrations, of all our British freshwater species.

## Wear Polaroid lenses 103

Never go chubbing without Polaroid glasses. I much prefer those with HLT, yellow lenses (high light transmission lenses), which make viewing in dull, overcast conditions noticeably brighter. Only in extra bright sunshine would I swap them for grey or amber lenses. A cap with a long peak stops you moving your hand up and down to shield your eyes from the sun. Less movement whilst fish spotting results in more chub in the net.

## Waterproof overtrousers 104

Invest in a good-quality, lightweight pair of waterproof overtrousers. You'll need them when kneeling, and crawling along Indian style, even during those early summer mornings when marginal grasses are soaked with dew.

## Use slugs as chub bait 105

Learn to keep a sharp look-out for slugs during early morning trips, especially when it's drizzling. During the summer and autumn, there is no finer, more instant chub bait than a big brown or black slug, hooked once only through either end on a size 4 hook tied direct to a 6lbs reel line, and free-lined (no additional shots) alongside those difficult 'snag' swims. Watch the line from the second the slug hits the water. Most bites quickly tighten the line like a bowstring, such is the ferocity of the take.

## Mind your fingers 106

Never put your finger down a chub's throat to ease out a large eyed hook. Your forefinger will come out (after a loud yelp of pain) looking like it's been hit with a 3lbs hammer. Why? Because chub have large, powerful pharyngeal (throat) teeth, that's why!

## Chub or Carp? 107

How do you tell the difference between a chub and a grass carp? The chub's mouth is much larger, and the eye of the grass carp is set very low, in line with its jaw hinge. In addition, the grass carp's anal fin is grey whilst the chub's has an orange hue. Otherwise, at a quick glance, especially in the water, they appear similar.

## Floating plugs 108

Enjoy weedy, seemingly impossible river conditions during the summer months with chub by catching them off the top on floating plugs. Good patterns are Big S style plugs, Meadow Mouse and Big Bud. Weedless models are particularly effective. Use a short wire trace to alleviate being bitten off by the occasional pike.

## Try mashed bread in winter 109

By far the best winter feed for chub is mashed bread. Use stale scraps soaked in the sink and squeeze most of the water out before mashing between your fingers into a pulp. The secret is that if old bread is used, it will sink quickly and break up into a million tiny fragments; thus attracting but not overfeeding.

## Little baits, big chub 110

Don't be surprised if you catch a big chub on small live baits intended for pike, perch or zander. They are one of our most voracious freshwater predators. Try ledgering minnows or bleak, dead or alive, and also half-inch chunks of eel or lamprey, which work well during the winter months. Loose feed sparingly with the same.

## Bending for chub 111

When long trotting for chub during the winter once the river bed has been scoured clean, use a wide-topped float (that can be easily seen up to 30-40 yards away) carrying a bulk shot of between 3-4 swan shots, but don't use swan shots. Instead bulk a line of AA shots 12-15 inches above the hook with a BB shot in between, so that just like a bath chain, the line of smaller shots bend without pulling the float under, whenever the river bed shallows up. See diagram.

Tip 111

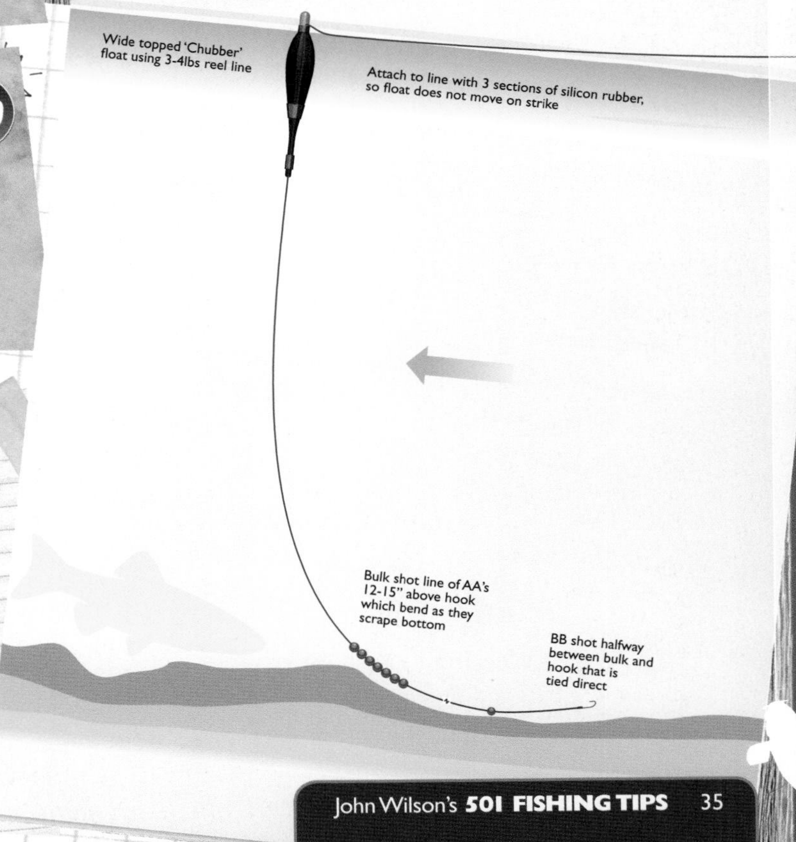

Freshwater Species

# Chub

## 112 Unhook carefully

Be careful using long nosed-artery forceps when unhooking deeply hooked chub. It is so easy to crimp and severely weaken the line immediately above the hook. If in any doubt, simply tie the hook on again.

## 113 Paternosters

For a simple way of constructing a fixed paternoster ledger (which suffices for most of my static-bait chub fishing), use the four-turn water knot. Cut off 10 inches of reel line (or weaker if fishing amongst snags) and join to the main line 18-24 inches above the end. Tie the hook on last.

## 114 Magic wasp cakes

When chub in a clear flowing river are particularly finicky during the warmer months, procure a whole wasp (or hornet's) nest. Try the pest control department of your local council, or get your own, but be careful (shop bought preparations are available) and slowly bring chub upstream into a feeding frenzy close to the surface by loose feeding chunks of £2 coin-sized wasp nest (called cake) which includes grubs. When most of the shoal is up on the surface inhaling every piece you drift down (it floats), put your hook in the next and free line on weightless tackle. You can virtually select which fish you want. Wasp cake is truly magical bait, and the large, succulent, white grubs can even be long-trotted one or two up on a size 12 hook whilst loose feeding with maggots.

## 115 Chub love nymphs

Summer chub are absolute suckers on the fly rod for large imitative nymphs presented upstream into the gravel runs they occupy between long flowing beds of weed. Get well below a shoal and offer a mayfly nymph on a long leader, remembering to recover line whilst watching it drift downstream. Strike at any unusual movement of the leader where it enters the water.

## 116 Bolt-rigging

To bag up on chub using the bolt-rig style approach of a heavy running bomb, stopped 8-12 inches from the hook. Use a short 3/4-1 inch hair baited with a single 10-14mm pellet or boilie, or two siz 10mm boilies or pellets, 3 grains of maize etc, while loose feeding with smaller attractor pellets, maize or sweetcorn. For distance or really deep-water swims, pack loose feed plus the occasional hook bait samples into PVA tubing or bags and nick onto the bend of the hook, which will dissolve within minutes.

## Easy weigh-ins 118

Don't bother using a separate weigh sling to weigh your specimen chub. If in the landing net it is already in a perfect receptacle. Simply unscrew the net top and hook it onto your scales, remembering to deduct its weight afterwards. What could be easier and less harm to the fish?

## Remaining focused 117

When ledgering across the flow in fast rivers, beware of those drop-back bites where a chub moves towards you and thus makes the quiver tip spring back. In most cases it is not your bomb, feeder or link ledger shots re-settling on the bottom. It is a chub. So strike instantly.

## Downstream at 45 degrees 119

When downstream quiver-tipping or rod top ledgering, angle your rod pointing downriver with the flow at around 45 degrees to the bank, as opposed to out at right angles. You will then pick up much more line on the strike, and even connect with tiny indications that would otherwise be missed.

## Mixer biscuits 120

When chub become suspicious of floating crust, step down to smaller offerings like mixer biscuits that you would use for carp. And simply present one super-glued onto a size 10 hook (don't forget to cut a small groove in the biscuit with a junior hacksaw blade first) using a small controller float 3-4 foot above for casting distance, stopped by a small rubber cushioning bead and a 5-turn stop knot tied on with a few inches of reel line. See Carp Tip 45.

## Be a creep 121

Concealment, stealth and camouflage are not just well-worn words of hype from angling writers. They are the basic requirements to successful chubbing, particularly when exploring and slowly stalking clear and shallow, overgrown rivers and streams. So always creep about below the skyline, using the screen of tall grasses, shrubs and trees to full advantage. And above all, move slowly. It is that sudden movement which instantly puts a wary chub on its guard.

# Eel

## Use lobworms 122

With large eels in mind, one of the most successful baits is a couple of lobworms presented on a size 4 hook, particularly in lakes or pits situated miles from the nearest river which contain only small numbers of adult eels (often referred to as 'prison waters). It was in fact this very bait that produced the long-standing British record eel of 11lbs 2oz back in 1978 to the rod of Steve Terry.

## Large bore run ring 123

As large eels are most sensitive to resistance, incorporate a large bore run ring into your running ledger rig. Use a lightweight indicator such as a simple coil of silver (kitchen) foil on the line between reel and butt ring, with an electric bite alarm as the front rod rest. Strong runs should then develop from an open bale arm.

## At night 124

Hot, humid, pitch-blac
thundery summer
nights provide the bes
opportunity of contacti
sizeable eels, which at
such times, often go o
a feeding rampage.

## Pools 125

In running water, by fa
the best locations for
targeting larger than
average sized eels are
weir and mill pools. Bu
you'll need substantial
tackle in pools where th
bottom is full of junk,
beneath which eels hav
their hideouts. This is
hold and wind' fishing
its most exciting.

## Watch for colour change 126

During the autumn, vast numbers of eels silver-up in readiness for their down-river migration and journey to procreate their species way across the Atlantic in the depths of the Sargasso Sea. Apart from a distinct change in colour from yellowy, greeny-brown, to bright silver, their jaws noticeably broaden and become more powerful. They thicken-up too.

## Use Kevlar materials 127

Big eels can at times chew through even 10lbs test monofilament. So construct your hook traces from one of the new soft, multi-strand, Kevlar-twisted materials marketed especially for catfish enthusiasts. Alternatively, use a thin, multi-strand wire that is so supple it can be knotted.

## Norfolk babbing 128

Though not a sports-fishing technique, babbing can provide a few hours fun during the hours of darkness, for anglers boat fishing during the summer months on eel-rich waters such as the Norfolk and Suffolk Broads.

## Babbing essentials 129

To babb effectively, you need several dozen large lobworms, a ball of wool (Worstead is best), and a long darning needle. Thread the worms onto the wool and wrap around your hand to form a wrap. Secure the ends tightly around the wrap and tie onto 10-12 foot of strong cord (100lbs test braid is ideal) with a 2-3 ounce lead fixed a foot or so above the worms. Then tie to the end ring of an 11-12 foot (light to hold) shore rod.

## Babbing technique 130

When babbing, the wrap of worms are lowered down to the river bed, followed by the rod tip vibrating continually once eels are chewing on the worms. And, because their teeth catch in the woollen yarn, they can be gently heaved out and lowered, all in one smooth, movement, straight into a large plastic bin. Don't worry about those that fall off. It's all part of babbing. You then have the choice of eating them immediately (simmering in milk in a saucepan produces a succulent meal of eel sections once they have been skinned) or freezing down for later use, either as sea baits for bass and tope, or for pike and zander.

## Befriend a netsman 131

If you happen to be friendly with a professional eel netsman, there is no better or more informed person to point you in the direction of a big-eel water: a still water containing catchable numbers of specimen eels which are in the 4lbs-plus category. Purchasing a batch of smaller eels from him to freeze down as winter pike baits might loosen his tongue.

# Eel

## Feeding times 132

Whilst eel fishing is invariably much better at night when they come out to play, the eels inhabiting deep reservoirs and gravel pits are likely to hunt, and consequently feed, at any time of the day, particularly during low light conditions.

## All through action rods 133

Use a powerful, but 'all through action' rod when targeting eels. It should bend in harmony with a 10-15lbs test monofilament reel line, and so not cause the hook to rip out, or induce the trace to fracture when the eel comes close in under the rod tip It should also be on a short line, ready for netting.

## Catching big eels 134

Prison waters invariably contain the largest freshwater eels of all. Lakes or ponds, modest-sized irrigation reservoirs or pits (even the tiniest of farm ponds) that are miles from the nearest river or brook. Such waters may not have been reached by many eels during their upstream migration, but those which made it are likely to grow to a very large size, due to minimal competition for food.

## Know when to move on 135

Many prison waters, especially small pits and farm ponds, give their best results during your initial few trips simply because they contain so few (albeit large) eels. So if results dwindle rapidly after say two or three trips, accept the fact that you may well have either caught, pricked, lost or simply scared virtually the water's entire eel population. So move on.

## Weighing in 136

To weigh your specimen eel (and anything from 4lbs upwards is a target fish), simply unscrew the landing net top and hoist onto the scales after removing the hook. Grip the eel firmly behind its head on the outside of the net, using the mesh as a gripping agent when extracting the hook. Then deduct the net's weight afterwards. It's so easy and much less slime is transferred from eel to you, than by attempting to transfer it into a separate weigh sling.

## Trophy shots 137

To take a trophy shot of a specimen eel, do so immediately after capture, unhooking when it is completely exhausted. If you leave in a sack or tube until dawn, by which time it will have recovered, taking any kind of decent photo will prove almost impossible.

## Scope the hideouts 138

In really large, still waters where feature hideout-habitats such as bridges, old boat houses, islands, dam walls, sunken boats or cars are evident, be prepared to move about and change swims regularly following every measure of success. This is because many of the very largest eels will occupy those choice habitat hideouts.

## Freshly killed baits 139

Do not be tempted into using large hook baits simply because you are seeking large eels. Big baits can cause more trouble than they are worth when it comes to deciding 'when' to strike a positive run. Small, slim-bodied, freshly killed fish such as gudgeon, bleak, dace, roach or rudd of between three and four inches in length are ideal. Odd ball baits like the entire insides of a large swan mussel, or a baby squid are also worth trying.

## Use a strong hook 140

To mount a small fish bait for optimum hook-ups, use a size 6-2 wide gape, strong hook, and push once only through the tail root. Work the hook along the baits flank (just beneath the skin) so it comes to lie immediately behind the gills with the point and bend of the hook nicely exposed. See Diagram. Just like pike, eels usually turn their prey to swallow head first so the fish's fins go down the gullet easily, and so a hook positioned immediately behind the gills usually finds purchase, despite the tail protruding from the eel's mouth. If you use a multi-hook rig, then use a wire trace in case a pike gobbles up your dead bait.

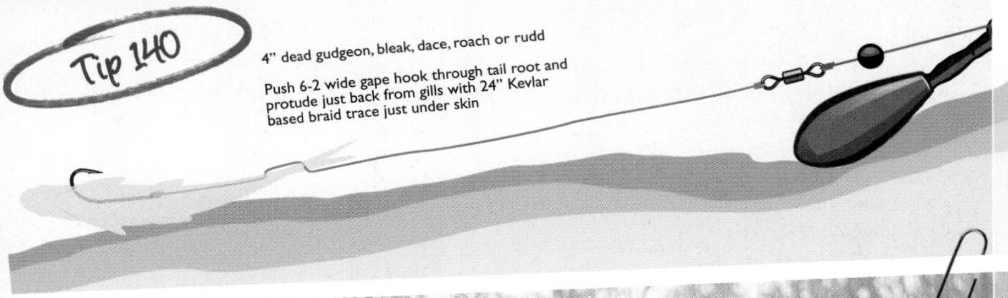

## The strike 141

When striking, close the reel's bale arm gently (vibrations might travel down the line) and point the rod directly at the eel, waiting for the line to pull tight. Then, in one smooth, easy action, haul the rod back into a full curve and start winding. Big eels immediately pull back using that inherent snake-like motion of their bodies, or actually run off. So make sure the clutch on your reel will yield line under pressure.

Freshwater Species

# Grayling

## BB shots 142

When long-trotting for her ladyship the grayling, do not be tempted to fish with too light a shotting pattern, or dot the float tip down as though stick-float fishing. Grayling are the boldest biters of all, even in the coldest weather. Wide-topped chubber-style floats that can easily be seen 30-50 yards downstream (yes, you can hit bites at such distances in fast water) carrying between two and five swan shots should do the job, but don't use swan shots. A line of AA-sized bulk shot pinched on 12 inches above a size 14, forged hook with a No 1 or BB shot half way between is far better, because like a bathroom chain, it bends when passing over stones and silt without pulling the float under, allowing the bait to drag bottom beautifully. See chub tip and diagram III.

## Male and female 143

Even in clear, cold water, grayling will pull the float down boldly so long as the bait is presented just above bottom, and within their line of sight. You can easily distinguish between male and female grayling by the different shapes of their dorsal fins. Males have a long sail-like dorsal, which when opened out almost touches their adipose fin, while females have smaller, almost square-shaped dorsals when opened out.

## In muddy waters 144

The only conditions when grayling won't play ball and bite confidently in cold weather is when the river is swollen over the banks full of dirty, milky-tea floodwater. They then seem loathe to move towards a trotted bait, perhaps on account that it cannot be seen clearly anyway. Switching over to stret-pegging tactics with two or three maggots, or a small red worm anchored hard on the river bed, and introducing loose feed directly down to the bottom by way of a bait-dropper, will sometimes produce. Also try quiver-tip ledgering in conjunction with a small block-end feeder rig.

## Freezing temps 145

After grayling, trout, pike, chub and dace (in that order) are the most likely species to bite in a freezing river. Remember that in sub-zero temperatures their metabolism will have slowed down to a snail's pace, and with chub and dace only tiny bite registrations are expected even t small static baits on tiny hooks, which is why trotting enthusiasts love grayling so much.

## Sweetcorn = salmon eggs 146

If you cannot get to a tackle shop in time for some maggots, or fail to find red worms in the compost heap, and you have a day's trotting for grayling already booked, then worry not. Grayling are real suckers for sweetcorn, trotted down just like maggots. It is thought that sweetcorn's resemblance in size to the eggs of salmon is what makes grayling accept it so readily. So it's always worth keeping a tin or two in the boot of your car, particularly coloured sweetcorn, which in orange looks uncannily like salmon eggs. Red works effectively too.

## Angling in chalk streams 147

Long trotting for grayling in clear-flowing southern chalk streams is not, as many seem to think, only for the privileged or the rich. The fishery managers and keepers of many highly-prized trout fisheries along rivers such as the Test and the Kennet, where grayling abound, actually encourage responsible anglers to enjoy this winter pursuit between the months of November and March. Simply enquire at tackle shops in towns like Stockbridge and Andover in Hampshire and in Newbury and Hungerford in Berkshire.

## End of season tip 148

As with big dace, there is very often a segregation of the sexes with grayling towards the end of the coarse fishing river season. This is in preparation of their eventual spawning during April, with the big males, being either loners or grouped in twos or threes, and now noticeably darker in colour, dominating many of the choice lies.

## Fly rodding for grayling 149

Summer or winter, grayling are always great fun to catch on the fly rod. With smaller, more intimate rivers in mind where short casting will cover most runs, a two ounce, wand-like carbon brook rod coupled to a lightweight reel and size 4 weight-forward floating line, allows the grayling to really show you what it can do. Use just a 2½-3lbs test tippet and plan to plop your artificial in at the head of each run (exactly where you would start trotting a float) from a position directly downstream. Plan to wade swims that demand it.

Freshwater Species

# Grayling

## Try weighted patterns 150

When fly fishing upstream for grayling, weighted patterns like the leaded shrimp and tin head or gold head nymphs on size 10 hooks are favourites. You need to be continually retrieving the loose line, as the nymph comes back downstream towards you with the current, your eyes glued to where the leader enters the surface, because sometimes you'll get little more than a quick forward twitch to pull into.

## Use a sight-bob 151

Many fly fishermen attach a buoyant, highly visible sight-bob to the leader 2-6 feet above the fly (depending on depth of the run being covered), which in effect acts just like a float and registers a bite instantly a grayling inhales the artificial.

## Breathable chest waders 152

Whether long trotting or presenting the upstream nymph to grayling during the winter months, it's worth investing in a pair of good-quality, lightweight, breathable chest waders with neoprene feet as opposed to rubber boots. They will allow you to sit comfortably low down on the bank side, kneel when required, or easily wade into a prime casting position, even wade fully across the river in order to cover choice swims along the opposite bank. Brogue-type leather or canvas wading boots with felt soles are then worn over the neoprene sock feet, providing excellent support for either wading over slippery stones in fast currents, or wandering along the banks.

## Travel light 153

The wandering, exploring grayling angler carries neither holdall nor tackle bag. All tackle sundries, such as fly boxes, floats, silicon float bands, hooks, shots, disgorger and forceps etc, are carried on his person in a waistcoat. A waistcoat with a tab and D ring on the back to accept the clip of a collapsible flick-up type landing net suits both the fly fisherman and long-trotter alike. There are times, however, when predominantly bank fishing over wide beds of reed and sedge, that a separate long handled landing net is required by the long trotting enthusiast.

## The bait pouch 15

An indispensable item of tackle when long trotting for her ladyship the grayling, is a simple two-division bait pouch. One for maggots and the other to hold red worms or sweet corn. This belts around the waist and alleviates the necessity of continually having to open bait boxes with freezing cold finger tips, to say nothing of carrying said boxes. When tackling wide rivers, a catapult is handy too.

## e grayling splash 155

thern chalk streams have hatches of flies about every day of the calendar year, l you can differentiate between a trout l a grayling sucking down an emerging or ating adult insect by the type of splash it eates. Look for the perfectly round ring of e grayling feeding off the surface.

## Flies 156

Small dry flies, anything in the olive range are readily taken as are sedges and mayflies. A grey wulff is one of the better larger patterns when it comes to sizeable grayling.

## Bait droppers 157

A small lightweight plastic bait dropper is very handy for ensuring that loose feed goes directly down along the bottom of deep and extremely turbulent gravel runs. Otherwise, hand-fed maggots would shoot off in all directions and at all levels, scattering the shoal in the process.

## Quick results 158

The nice thing about grayling is that once the float has been set at the correct trotting depth to present the bait trundling along just above the river bed, there is little point in making any more than three or four trots through before moving on to the next run. If grayling are present, a bite will usually come at the first or second run through.

## Scope the fishery 159

When tackling the grayling of shallow and clear flowing chalk streams, first walk the entire fishery upon arrival, starting from the downstream boundary up. Make note of those swims which contain the most or the largest fish and where big trout or the odd salmon are lying, in order to avoid them. Do this all the way upstream to the top boundary. Then walk and fish the entire fishery downstream along which everything will by now have settled.

## The grayling playground 160

Top chalk stream features much loved by larger grayling are tiny, deep hatch pools, deep runs close into the bank, even those of just a few yards in length, and those long, even-paced, even-depth glides with a clean sandy bottom.

## Keep an eye on your hook 161

Be prepared during an exhaustive day's long trotting to change your hook several times. The tell-tale sign of your hook becoming blunt is when a maggot becomes difficult to impale or bursts as you nick it on.

Freshwater Species

# Perch

## Back ledgering 162

Of all top techniques for catching perch during the winter months, once the weed in lakes and rivers has died back, back-ledgering, is the most deadly, because through minimal casting it creates less disturbance. Go for a two rod-approach, employing a simple fixed paternoster ledger rig on each, with a couple of 2x or 3x swan shots (depending upon casting distance or current strength) on the 10 inch weight link, and a large, gyrating lobworm nicked onto a size 4, on the 20 inch hook length.

## Catapult bait 163

For back-ledgering in rivers (quiver-tip rods are actually recommended here because the fine, forgiving tips are less likely to pull the hook from a lightly hooked perch), cast one rod as far downstream as you can, and the second around half the distance. Catapult in several helpings of broken lobworms down the entire length of the swim between the far bait and the end of your near rod, to get the perch in a feeding mood. And continue introducing broken worms throughout the session when fish are coming regularly.

## Pointing at baits 164

When back-ledgering, both rods should be almost pointing at the baits. I say almost, because if set in the rests at a slight angle, gentle pulls and the start of a bite is often shown on the quiver tip before the bobbin actually moves. And so striking can be pre-empted. Then clip on a lightweight bobbin-type indicator between reel and butt ring. An electric bite alarm (used as a front rod rest incidentally), comes in very useful when sport is slow, and you don't want to miss out by day dreaming.

## Broken worms 165

Every 10-20 minutes or so, when back ledgering, remove the bobbin and gently lift up each rod whils winding the reel's handle between one and a couple of turns, thus moving the worm off the bottom (it will flutter down beautifully) towards you. Then put the rod down, wind up slightly and clip on th bobbin. A drop of around 12-14 inches is ideal. But sometimes you will barely have time for this beca a perch will have nailed your lobworm on the drop. Remember to keep those broken worms going in throughout the session, or bites may dry up.

# Big perch in still waters

166

Where do big perch live? Well, due to summer weeds dying back, when fry shoals tend to mass together for protection in deeper holes and gullies, larger perch then subsequently tend to group-up in catchable numbers close by. So in still waters such as lakes and gravel pit complexes, if you are not aware of the water's bottom topography, spend some time plumbing the depths to locate those choice, deeper areas. Marginal features such as an old boat house built adjacent to deep water, beneath overhanging and part-sunken trees and dam outlets, are also worth exploration.

# Perch in river systems

167

Look for top-habitat swims, where large bushes and trees overhang the water, especially where willows dunk their lower limbs below the surface. Keep an eye out for those big perch-swims par excellence: beds of dense bull rushes. Both habitats harbour perch because they provide great ambush points. The dark, vertical stripes of the perch blend in perfectly with the stems of the bulrush and with the subsurface stems of the willow. Around lock gates, beneath road bridges and beside pilings are also favoured, as are the holes on acute bends and cut-backs along thick beds of sedges hugging the margins. Also, see Tips 173 and 174.

# atch the weather patterns

168

rious big-perch specialists are very selective about when they , and keep a keen track of winter weather patterns. Because le perch are possibly likely to feed at any time regardless of peratures, by far the hottest feeding periods occur during lls of extra-mild weather. Wait until temperatures do not fall ow zero for several consecutive nights, rising to maybe 10 or 12 grees during the day, and get out there pronto.

# Small live baits

169

When ledgering small live-baits for perch (gudgeon, dace, roach and little perch are best - in that order), I favour a reel line of around 6lbs test matched to an Avon-style ledger rod of 11-12 feet. On the business end is tied a wide-gape size 4 eyed hook, to 20 inches of reel line and a small swivel. Above this goes a cushioning rubber bead and a running snap swivel with 4 inch heavy mono 'link' and one ounce bomb attached. Any lighter and the bait might tow the lead around.

# Rod angles

170

Always angle the rod tip downwards supported on two rests and pointing directly at the bait to minimise resistance when ledgering small live baits. For bite indications, hang a simple bobbin on a 20 inch drop between reel and butt ring, pinching a swan shot or two on the retaining cord to counteract excessive movement from the bait.

# Rubber bands

171

To ensure the single hook is not impaired on the strike when live baiting, hook the bait fish once only through its chin membrane or both nostrils, and slip on over the barb, a 1/4 inch square of rubber band. This alleviates the bait flying off during the cast or at any other time.

# Perch

## Big perch, little perch 172

The old saying that 'the best bait to catch a big perch, is a little perch', is on most occasions, perfectly true. Next to gudgeon, which seem to possess magical powers of attraction to big stripies, a small, live perch of around 4-5 inches long is indeed hard to beat because large perch become so, by consuming large quantities of their own brethren in addition to other small silver-shoal species.

## Hunt down the bulrushes 173

Just like barbel, river perch adore bulrushes. Not those tall dark brown, cigar-like seed heads of the greater reed mace, often wrongly referred to as bulrushes, but the cylindrical, dark-green onion-like stems which protrude through the surface from a gravel bed. This can often be seen quivering often in huge marginal clumps as well as through the middle of a shallow river, as the strong current bows them slightly over.

## Using small, live baits 174

It is most important to differentiate between bulrushes and reed mace because they each prefer different habitats. Perch love true bulrushes because their vertical stripes blend in remarkably well with the erect stems, affording them marvellous ambush opportunities, from where they can attack small silver shoal species, using minimum effort. But if you cannot obtain small live baits don't worry. A juicy lobworm or dendrobena trotted along just above bottom beneath an Avon-style or chubber float produces the most gloriously positive bites. Free lining a big worm into gaps between the bulrushes, and allowing it to free-fall to the bottom as it drifts along will also produce aggressive chub-like bites; the line zinging tight after a preliminary twitch or two.

## Over-fed perch 175

One of the best or worst-kept secrets about commercial carp-type fisheries, is the size the perch, if stocked, grow to. Specimens over 3lbs are common place, due to the amount of loose feed in the way of casters, maggots and worms that are used to attract carp and silver shoal species. If you add the fry of silver shoal species that breed in these albeit small, but prolific waters, you don't have to be a rocket scientist to realise that commercial water perch are extremely well fed. Reason enough to be the odd man out by specifically targeting them.

## mple paternosters 176

e-roaming live baits all too easily dive into ed or beneath trees or vacate the area all gether when predators show up. A simple nning paternoster ledger rig presented neath a small (through the middle) sliding oat is the best way of live baiting for big perch, ecause it keeps your bait continually working ver the targeted area.

## Sliding floats 177

To rig a sliding float (using a tiny bead and five-turn stop knot above), set it a little deeper than the swim, with the 6lbs test main line threaded through one end of a swivel and tied to the hook link swivel (with a small bead between) and a wide gape size 4 on the business end of the 16 inch hook length. To the loose swivel above the bead (which now becomes the bomb link), tie 20-30 inches of 8lbs mono and add a one ounce bomb. Small roach, rudd, gudgeon and dace, are ideal baits and work continually if simply hooked through both nostrils. Remember to angle the rod top high in order to keep as much line out of the water as possible.

## End of season 178

To stand a chance with the largest perch of all, concentrate on the species during the last few weeks of the river fishing season leading up to the middle of March when, due to increased temperatures, they will be looking to feed heavily prior to their eventual spawning during April.

## Forget wire trace 179

Don't be tempted to hedge your bets whilst offering live baits to perch by incorporating a wire trace in case a pike happens along. Perch, the whoppers especially, are particularly sensitive to a wire trace. Besides, should a pike bite through your 6lbs reel line, it will either quickly get rid of a large single, bronze hook, or the hook will rot and rust away within weeks.

## Weir pool sills 180

During the warm summer months, you will find big river perch below the churning, well oxygenated white water of a weir pool, immediately below the sill and in the corresponding eddies on both sides. Vast shoals of newly hatched fry gather in such places and perch are only too aware of the fact. Try a small diving plug or float-fished live bait like a bleak or a gudgeon set around mid-depth. Your float won't be on the surface for too long.

## Easy does it 181

Beware of striking float-fished live baits too hard. Simply tighten down once the float has disappeared and wind up tight until you can feel the fish. Then pull the rod tip back and wind in one smooth movement, continuing to wind so the hook finds purchase as the perch tries to eject the bait by shaking its head from side to side.

Freshwater Species

# Pike

## 182 Handling and unhooking

To handle pike safely and carefully for both a trophy photo and during the process of unhooking, use a chain mail glove on your left hand (the Rapala Fillet Glove is perfect for the job and will fit either hand). Gently slip four fingers into the pike's left gill opening, being very careful not to touch its gill rakers. When your fingers are fully in, press down tightly on the outside (against your forefinger) with your thumb. Don't relax your grip or the fish might escape. To remove hooks with long nosed-artery forceps (imperative), simply curl your left hand slowly, and 'hey presto' the pike's lower jaw will open. It has no option because being part of its bony skull the top jaw has little movement anyway. It really is so easy, and small fish can even be unhooked with most of their body still in the water, or when held vertically. For maximum support, big fish are best laid on their back on an unhooking mat during the unhooking process. Hooks deep down are most easily removed by going in with the forceps through the opposite gill opening.

## 183 High-visibility sliding pike floats

When float fishing at distance in still water, use 'hi-viz' sliding pike floats that incorporate dart-type sight-vanes, and remember to use 3-4mm rubber cushioning beads either side of the float, between floa eye and trace swivel. Use another bead between float eye and a sliding stop knot, tied onto the reel line above the float at the required depth, using a few inches of 10-15lbs test, red (easy to see) power gum. Don' trim the ends too short (leave both 1 1/2 inches long) or the knot will catch against the rod rings during casting and inhibit distance.

## 184 The weigh-in and trophy shot

To weigh trophy-sized pike, it's far easier immediately after landing when they are still in the folds of a large (already wet) net. One with arms around 40-42 inches in length will accommodate the biggest specimens, and you simply detach the arms from the spreader block and roll the net up before hooking the scales on halfway along, remembering to deduct the weight of the net afterwards. What could be easier? Then lay the pike onto a foam-filled unhooking mat, either still in or out of the landing net, and remove the hooks. A separate weigh sling is really not required. Now is the time for a photo, following unhooking, immediately prior to release when they are at their quietest. Don't try to retain a large pike in a keep-sack or tube for any length of time in order to capture a picture of it. Truth is, once pike have regained their strength by resting in a sack, they become unbelievably difficult to hold still. And at best you will become heavily covered in their protective slime as they wriggle about. So for the sake of both pike and angler, immediate release is always recommended.

## Mr Pike the predator

185

Some anglers tend to think that pike should be shown less stealth than the chub. This is because the pike is a marauding killer with an enviable array of backward-pointing teeth covering the roof of its upper jaw, in addition to the long, powerful canines set into the lower jaw and thus capable of engulfing, drowning and swallowing water birds as large as mallards. However, this is wrong. So acute are the senses of pike, even totally blind fish are confident at lunging into a shoal of bait fish or striking at an artificial lure. Smelling out static dead baits resting on the bottom is by comparison, child's play of course. This predator has in fact survived in British rivers and lakes for at least half a million years. Fossil remains found in Germany date back to 20 million years ago.

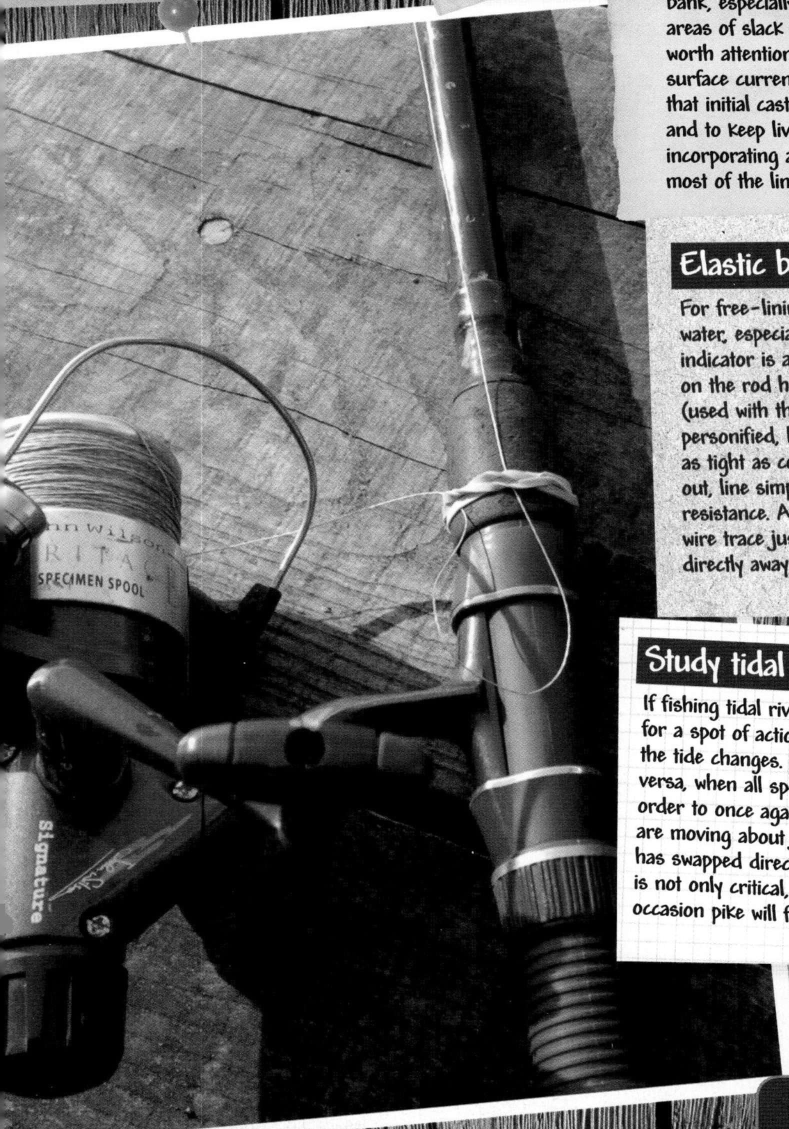


## Tempting hungry pike

186

Mill and weir pools are great meeting places for all river species. And because the occupants must keep moving in the fast currents, they need to feed more regularly, even throughout the coldest winter conditions; pike included. In water running low and clear, best results usually come to trotted live baits just above bottom, or working lures. A big spoon is my favourite, which with just the one treble hook at the rear, catches up on fewer snags than say, diving plugs. Wobbling dead baits is another extremely effective weir pool technique, which maximises on time because you don't have to catch live baits first. And while a pike is likely to turn up anywhere except the main flush, I favour any slow back eddy close into the bank, especially those lies beneath overhanging trees. Small areas of slack water beneath redundant hatch gates are also worth attention, as are any areas of slow, deep water. So, study surface currents seriously for several minutes before making that initial cast. Sometimes slacks occur in the pools centre, and to keep live bait out there use a float-paternoster rig incorporating a heavy bomb, and angle the rod tip high to keep most of the line off the surface between float and tip.

## Elastic band indicator

187

For free-lining dead baits to pike in both still and running water, especially when boat fishing, the most effective bite indicator is a loop of line retained beneath an elastic band on the rod handle immediately opposite the reel's spool (used with the reel's bale arm open). This is sensitivity personified, because you can make the band as forgiving or as tight as conditions dictate and once the loop has pulled out, line simply peels from the spool without the slightest resistance. Always pinch a couple of swan shots onto the wire trace just below the swivel to initiate the pike moving directly away and giving a positive bite indication.

## Study tidal change

188

If fishing tidal rivers for pike, remember the most likely time for a spot of action particularly when sport is slow, is when the tide changes. Either from flooding to the ebb or visa versa, when all species including pike must change position in order to once again face the flow. And that period when fish are moving about just before the change, to when the river has swapped direction and is flowing in the opposite direction, is not only critical, on a bad day it is very often the only occasion pike will find your baits.

Freshwater Species

# Pike

## My spoon and static approach

189

If you are fed up with waiting for one of the baits presented on a multiple-rod set-up to be taken, try my spoon and static approach. A highly mobile technique I employ when searching previously un-fished rivers and lakes for pike, guaranteed to keep you warm. I use two 9 foot rod outfits, one of which sports a fixed spool reel (could be a multiplier) loaded with 12lbs mono, plus wire trace and a 5 inch spoon. The second reel is a 6501-sized (left-hand wind) multiplier loaded with 30lbs test braid and wire trace holding a duo of size 8 semi barb-less trebles. I start by selecting a likely area, pinch two 2x swan shots onto the wire trace immediately below the swivel, fix on dead bait such as a smelt, mackerel tail, or whole sardine, and cast it out. Once the bait has touched bottom, I lay the rod on the ground pointing at the bait, without worrying about rod rests and bite indicators and wind the loose line reasonably tight. The reel is then clicked into free spool and the ratchet engaged. This is my audible bite indicator. I then search the surrounding territory with the spoon-outfit, retrieving it close to the bottom in an erratic, fluttering, wounded-fish action, with the rod tip pointing directly at the lure to maximise on the hooks going home when a pike lunges at it. I'll spend no more than say 15-20 minutes in any spot, before twitching the static back (in case it gets grabbed on the move) and then move on to the next likely swim. There are days when pike really want a chase and the fluttering spoon scores, and times when only the static is taken, usually quite quickly too, within 5-10 minutes of being cast. And of course there are days when both methods produce.

## Try small baits for big pike

190

Now here is a really top, top tip. That old adage of offering a 'big' bait if you are after a big pike, does not necessarily add up. Often with larger baits, the problems of hooking-up are far greater. Personally, whether live or dead baiting, I much prefer whole fish or half baits in the 5-7 inch size bracket. I can then point the rod at the pike and wind down till the line is completely tight, before striking immediately, all in one progressive action, knowing that I have more than a fair chance of the hooks finding purchase.

## Use aromas and blood saturated fish

191

For ledgering static dead baits in deep, fast, coloured rivers, use aromatic species such as the cucumber smelling smelt and grayling, or blood-saturate fish like lampreys and eels, especially the head-ends that have huge blood content. Mackerel and herring heads also work very well. Initial knocks on the rod tip (which should be angled up high to ensure maximum line is out of the water) signal a pike mouthing the bait, after which line will evaporate quickly from the reel. So either use a multiplier in free spool with the ratchet on, a loop of line set tightly beneath an elastic band on the rod handle with the reel's bale arm open, or a bait-runner reel. Alternatively, the rod tip might suddenly spring back denoting a pike has dislodged the ledger weight whilst taking the bait. If the line fails to pull from the reel, it's because the pike has swum towards the rod. So wind down instantly, and feel for that tell-tale knocking of a fish already on.

Tip 192

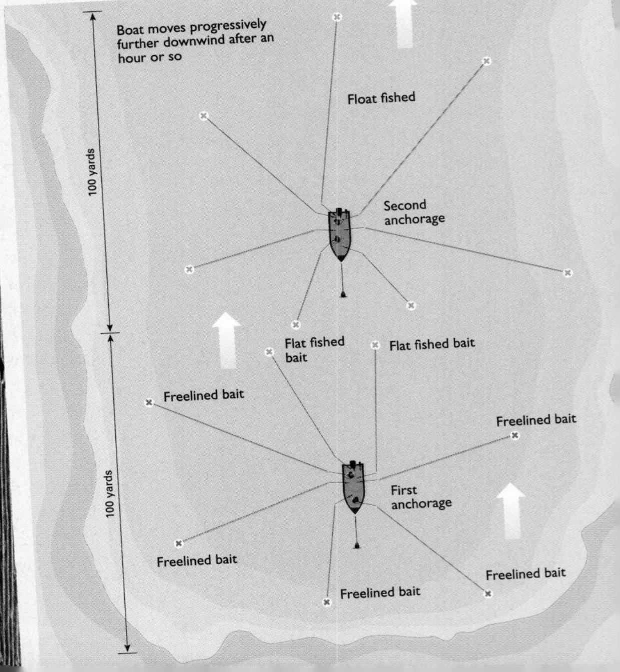

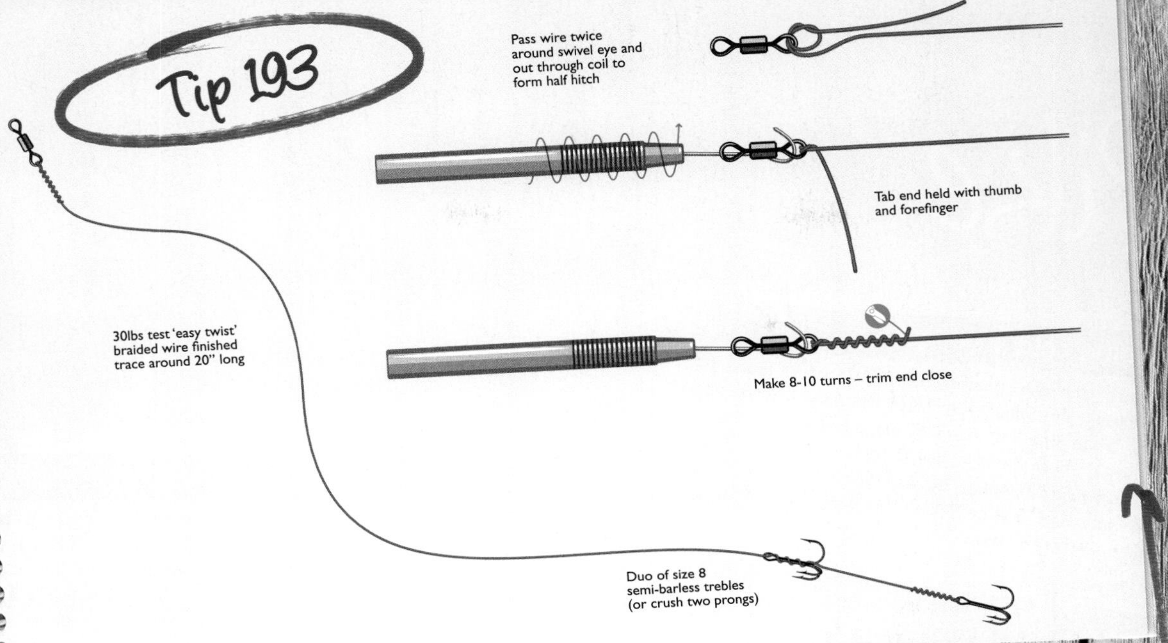


## For the middle reaches 192

When targeting the big pike of my local Norfolk Broads during the coldest, most featureless time of the year (December to March), a large percentage of the fish I'm after will be well out from the bank on the bottom of the bowl (many of the shallower broads are like a saucer in cross-section) in the deepest section. For this kind of pike fishing, I find that systematically grid-searching the middle reaches of the broad, pays best dividends. After putting the mud weights down at the most upwind area, rods are fanned all around the boat presenting static dead baits. Use a mixture of float-fished and free-lined smelt and lamprey heads, with the tip of each rod pointing directly at the bait. The idea is to cover every angle of where a pike might be lying or approach the bait from. If nothing materializes within say an hour after repositioning each bait a couple or three times, then lift the mud weights silently and try the next area downwind. This technique certainly produces a high proportion of quality-sized double figure fish (not to mention the occasional whopper), which show a distinct preference for static dead baits. See diagram opposite.

## Make your own traces 193

Fancy making up your own traces for pike? Not only is it cheaper than purchasing tackle shop pre-mades, but you have total choice in what patterns of hooks and swivels are used, plus the type of wire they are presented on. And if the trace lets you down, you only have yourself to blame. But because making your own is so much cheaper, you will automatically replace each one immediately it becomes doubtful through fraying or bent hooks. Essential items include a selection of trebles and swivels (may I suggest size 10 swivels and size 8 semi barb-less trebles will suffice for most pike fishing), a roll of 30lbs test easy-twist braided wire, and a small pair of quality wire cutters. A twiddle stick, which has a shepherd's crook at one end for twisting the tab end of the wire around itself, to secure treble or swivel (though this can be done with your bare fingers) not only makes constructing traces easier, but more professional-looking too. See diagram above. Start by cutting off around 24 inches of wire and (assuming you are right-handed) holding a treble in your left hand, with your right, pass one end of the wire through the eye, and then a second time to form a loop. Now pass the end through the loop to form a simple clinch and gently pull evenly on both strands of wire to reduce the loop into a tight knot. Using your left hand, catch the crook of the twiddle stick around one prong of the treble and slowly revolve towards you, whilst with your right hand (holding the tab end of wire between thumb and forefinger) carefully guide it around itself in neat coils. After a dozen or so coils, snip off the end. Slide on the second treble (through the eye) and secure two to three inches above the first treble by gently wrapping the wire three or four times around the shank. To complete the trace, repeat the twisting procedure by adding a swivel to the other end. And there it is. Job done. Traces end up around 20 inches long (after twisting and trimming) so that should the bottom few inches of wire become kinked or frayed after catching a pike or two, cutting off the suspect length of wire and replacing the trebles takes but a jiffy. And your trace is still long enough for action, though a few inches shorter. Make up spinning traces (12-14 inches long) with a plain swivel at one end and a snap swivel at the other, in exactly the same way.

Freshwater Species

# Pike

## 194 Catching cold water pike

To ensure your lure or wobbled dead bait works only within this critical, cold-water depth band, less than two feet above bottom, try adding a 12 inch stiff mono link and running swivel immediately above the trace swivel (with a small bead between) with a half ounce bomb on the end. You can then twitch and wobble your dead bait or lure in ever so slowly, only tightening up when you feel a take.

## 195 Sliding tenpin floats

When trotting down live or dead baits for river pike, use an in-line, sliding, Tenpin-style buoyant float. The reel line passes through this and is stopped at the desired depth by a small bead and five-turn stop knot, tied with power gum. Bulk shot in the way of two to three large swan shots or a large oval bullet (cushioned by a rubber bead) should sit on the main line immediately above the trace swivel. The beauty of using the sliding Tenpin is that at any point along the swim where the bottom is known to shallow up or there is a snag, you simply ease the stop knot a few feet above the float by holding the rod tip high, and then let it go again when depth resumes. In addition, this is the perfect rig for stret-pegging dead baits static on the bottom of fast flowing rivers.

## 196 Flat floats

To rig the sliding tenpin or any other 'through the middle' pike float for stret-pegging, simply exchange the shots or oval bullet for a running 1-2 ounce bomb, and slide the stop knot up to several feet deeper than the swim. Then cast directly downstream, and allow a subsurface bow to form in the line between float and terminal rig, so that the float actually lies flat on the surface. The flat float creates minimal resistance to a pike sucking up the bait.

## 197 Use rainbow trout

Want the most durable of all baits to use for a day's wobbling for pike where continual and long casting are prerequisites? Well, look no further than 5 to 7 inch rainbow trout which have unbelievably firm bodies and last for ages. You can purchase them frozen from specialist tackle shops, or enquire at your local trout farm or fishery where small disfigured and freshly dead trout are removed daily from the stews. When mounted on a duo of size 8 semi barb-less trebles (the top in an eye socket and the lower down the flank) with a slight bend set in the trout's body, a lovely action is produced.

## ...pping up dead bait 198

...popping-up light, whole dead baits such as roach, smelts or sprats ...ve bottom silt and weed, simply twist a 2-3 inch link of soft multi- ...nd wire onto to the shank of the lower treble on your standard ...-hook wire trace. Then, at the other end, twist-on a green 3/4 ... diameter Pro Popper soft foam buoyant ball to raise the bait's head ... torso off the bottom. Pinch a 2 or 3x SSG shot onto the wire trace ...v inches from the bait's tail (to ensure it rises the exact distance ...red above bottom) and another next to the trace swivel. It works ...bsolute treat, and pike are not put off, because the foam ball is soft. ...opping up larger baits, simply use two small foam balls, instead of ...arger one, which could impair striking.

## When looking for huge pike... 199

When after the huge pike of trout reservoirs, there are two kinds of fish-holding features to look for: visual features such as valve towers, the dam wall and around the cages where trout are fed daily in the floating stews; and unseen features, which only become apparent when using an echo-sounder/fish-finder unit. These might consist of anywhere that dense shoals of baitfish gather such as around an old stone wall (many reservoirs, remember, are flooded farmlands) or group of buildings, or the deeper bed of a stream or river, rocky outcrops, defunct farm machinery. The possibilities are endless, and all will show up on the finder.

## ...ght pike 200

...e you ever thought about fishing for pike at night? In ...e cases, particularly on waters heavily fished for pike, in ...n rivers and still waters, results can actually surpass those ...de during daylight. Dead baiting using simple ledgering ...ics, presenting static baits on the bottom, is by far the ...iest and most productive method. Pretend you are carp ...ing at night by using electric bite alarms and indicators, ...d by take along hot drinks and warm clothing, plus a ...werful torch and other necessities such as a towel and head ...p. Actually pre-baiting during the hours of darkness, areas ...t are popular during the day (see Ground baiting Tips 487 ...d 488) can make an enormous difference to your results. ... it and see.

## Fly fishing for pike 201

Ever tried fly fishing for pike? I should say fly-rodding really, because with pike, and to a much lesser extent other predatory species such as chub, perch and zander, flies are tied up to represent small fish, frogs, newts or small rodents – not flying insects. You need a fairly long (10 foot is ideal) powerful rod capable of throwing 9 and 10 weight lines, plus a large diameter fly reel, preferably with a sensitive disc drag. Add a floating, sinking and fast-sinking line, and you are there, but for a few short, supple wire traces (which become the leader tippet) plus an assortment of large flies and bugs. It's great fun too, and in shallow water especially, the turn of speed and subsequent tail-walking action from a fly-hooked pike can prove spectacular.

# Roach & Dace

## Try in low-light conditions 202

Being a shoal fish, roach are forever watchful of changing situations and circumstances that affect their brethren. This is why the entire shoal often stops feeding confidently at the drop of a hat (as though a switch has been pulled) when danger occurs. Like the sudden appearance of a pike in the swim, with its fins quivering (a sure sign of its intention to attack) or simply the sun suddenly hitting clear water at an angle that immediately illuminates everything. The shoal is merely relating to its vulnerability. This is why the biggest, wiliest roach of all, those over that magical 2lb bracket, whose fellow shoal members have diminished in numbers over the seasons through predation and disease, usually only feed with the utmost confidence in conditions of low light: at dusk and into darkness, and again at dawn. Time has taught them they are far less vulnerable and subsequently less likely to be attacked and eaten when their pursuers cannot see so well. A point well worth remembering.

## Quiver-tip ledgering 203

When you cannot buy a bite from river roach in cold winter conditions, it is because their metabolism has slowed down - they refuse to move quickly in order to intercept food on the move, no matter how juicy your maggots. Roach hate changing position every few seconds in really cold water and expending unnecessary energy. They much prefer to slowly suck up small particles of static food such as maggots from the river bed. So switch over to quiver-tip ledgering, using a small block-end feeder (to deposit loose feed with extreme accuracy beside your hook bait) and offer two maggots on a size 16 hook, stepping down to smaller hooks and a single maggot if bites are not forthcoming.

## Going for big dace 204

Want a really big dace? Something between, say, 12 ounces and that magical one pound figure? Then concentrate trotting maggots or small cubes of bread crust close to the bottom in the deeper, roachy-looking swims of smaller rivers, particularly chalk streams, during the last two weeks of the river fishing season in early March. Dace are often segregated by sex at this time, as an early grouping process prior to their eventual spawning during April. The big, pigeon-chested females rest up in the deeper, slower swims, while the males (already covered in spawning tubercles) decidedly wiry and sand-papery to hold, mass together along the fast, shallow reaches.

## Sensitive quiver tips 205

When ledgering using basic rigs with small baits presented on small hooks for roach and dace, it's imperative to employ the most sensitive of quiver-tip indicators. For those who do not own built-in, or push-in quiver tip rods of varying tip strengths, invest in a selection of screw-in quiver tips starting at one ounce test curve for really slow currents, going up to 2-2 1/2 ounces for rivers like the full-flowing Severn.

## Use moving baits 206

There is something extraordinarily satisfying about watching a strong flow whisk your red-topped float smoothly downstream. The current draws the 2lb-2 1/2lb test line steadily from a free-running centre pin reel, while you gently brake the side of the drum with thumb pressure, ensuring the bait is presented as near as possible to the actual current speed down there close to the bottom. Yes, searching for specimen-sized roach in running water is arguably the most rewarding of all ways to see a big one come sliding over your net. And by big, let's say roach of around 2lb and upwards, because being in a minority and rather scarce in these times of chronic cormorant predation, such fish are now highly prized. And to encourage one to intercept a moving bait (maggots, casters or a piece of fresh white bread flake), mild conditions coupled to a coloured river are essential. If long trotting, and the river's running crystal clear, you're unlikely to get a bite until the light fades, and then you have but a few casts remaining to score. But catch the river immediately following heavy flooding when visibility just starts to improve, but where you still lose sight of a maggot a foot below the surface, and those roach could well feed for at least a couple of hours. So make the most of mild spells and coloured water.

## Avoiding debris 207

To alleviate the annoyance of debris, both surface and down the line, when ledgering for roach and dace in a swollen river, you have two options. Either fish static mill or over-shoot pools that have backed up - often full of fish in the right conditions - or select swims immediately behind wide bridge supports, behind sunken trees or on the inside and immediately downstream of acute bends. In short, wherever fish group up to seek respite out of the main flow, and where the full force of the current is deflected away from your ledgered bait.

Freshwater Species

# Roach & Dace

## Bulking up — 208

To catch roach and dace using the waggler float, bulk most of the shotting capacity (say 75–85 percent) on each side of the bottom ring, leaving a 1/2 inch gap between for the float to fold smoothly on the strike. This not only allows dart-like accuracy when casting because the shots pull the float through the air, but also only the very minimum of shots are then required down the line to create a natural fall of the hook bait, which is most important when fishing in still waters. This leaves you free to add just a few small shots (No 6 and 8 shots are perfect) starting midway between float and hook. Then, if the rig happens to fold at the highest shot, the hook won't be able to touch the float or locking shots and tangle. For trotting in running water, larger shots can be used down the line, and an overall heavier bulk shotting in order that the bait trundles or drags along close to the bottom.

## Essential headgear — 209

Remember to have a peaked baseball-type cap or visor in your kit when float fishing for roach and dace in bright conditions. It is essential to stop you from squinting all day when concentrating upon the float tip.

## Silicon float adaptors — 210

When waggler fishing for roach in waters where you may need to change from straight to tipped or insert floats, or to models carrying a greater shotting load, attach the float to your line using a silicon float adaptor. Switching from one float to another then takes seconds.

## Shorten your hook tail — 211

When you're float fishing or ledgering for roach and dace and your maggots or casters repeatedly come back crushed, you have actually missed and perhaps not even seen, a positive bite. All cyprinid species including roach and dace are equipped with powerful pharyngeal teeth in the back of their throats, for masticating their food, and so to wind in sucked maggots means the fish has actually had your hook well inside its mouth. To remedy this so you can identify a bite, keep shortening your hook tail if ledgering, or if float fishing move the lowest shot closer to the hook until bites are registered. Also, shoot the float tip down so it's a mere 'blimp' in the surface film (this is imperative in cold conditions).

## Electrician's tape 212

When ledgering for roach and dace in fast flowing rivers using a block-end feeder rig, you don't want maggots or casters emptying too quickly. So keep a roll of black electrician's tape in your kit, so you can slow down the rate of release by taping up some of the holes. Simple, but effective.

## Quick feeder changes 213

Regardless of which type of feeder you start the day with, make sure it is attached to your lead-link via a tiny snap link swivel. Then you can change the size and type of your feeder, literally within seconds.

## Pinching on bread flake 214

When using bread flake on the hook, do not pinch it on too hard, especially when long trotting, otherwise hook penetration at distance becomes a problem. Pinch only a small area of the flake (around the eye of the hook) on hard, allowing the rest to swell into an attractive carnation around the hook.

## Luminous elements at night 215

For quiver-tip ledgering at night, you will want to watch a powerful beta light element, or one of the extra-bright chemical luminous elements. Both of these can be sleeved into a short length of clear tubing pushed onto a Tip-sight holder, which itself is sleeved into silicon tubing on the quiver tip immediately below the tip ring. First of all, a length of clear silicone tubing is sleeved over the tiny tip ring to accommodate the holder. For a more permanent fixture, the holder may be whipped to the quiver tip.

## ...or try a nightlight adaptor 216

An even easier way of adding a luminous element for night fishing, is by attaching an Enterprise Tackle nightlight adaptor. This ingenious piece of kit can literally be fitted in seconds, accommodates elements between 3.0 and 4.5mm in diameter in a short length of clear tubing and keeps the two halves of the unit (which actually hinges and folds around the quiver tip) held tightly together. These adaptors come two to a packet, one large and one small. The larger will also fit on rod tops up to 2mm in diameter.

## ...or go for a painted tip 217

If luminous elements fail to hold your attention for ledgering at night, then simply illuminate a white-painted quiver tip or rod top with a narrow torch beam. Position it from downstream, to angle outwards and upstream, thus illuminating only the quiver tip. It will then not impair your night-time vision, or shine into the water and scare the fish.

## Construct a mini ledger 218

To quickly construct a mini ledger, pinch a shot onto the line 10-18 inches above the hook, and immediately above fold a short length of slightly thicker line over the reel line. Pinch onto this sufficient shots to hold bottom, leaving a gap slightly narrower than the stop shot, so the ledger slides freely up the line.

Freshwater Species

# Roach & Dace

## Stick floating 219

To fish the stick float correctly, you need calm conditions, (a gentle upstream wind is sometimes advantageous) and all the shots should be evenly spaced (shirt-button style) between float and hook. For the most subtle presentation of small baits like a single maggot or caster, make the two shots closest to the hook smaller than the rest. See diagram below. The stick float works most effectively in depths from 4–10 feet, but only at short range with the tip dotted down to a mere 'blimp' in the surface film. A rod length and a half out, say. Do not allow any loose line between rod and float tip and get used to counting down and observing how many seconds it takes for all the shots to dot the tip of the float down to its final position, and strike instantly when it takes too long. One big shot may very well cock the same float instantly, but up to a dozen tiny shots will take several seconds, and this is your period for interpreting and striking into bites on the drop.

Tip 219

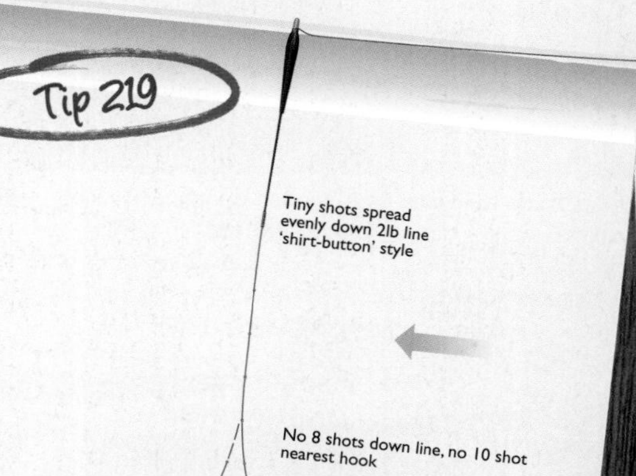


## Centre-pin reel 220

Of course not all bites will come on the drop when fishing the stick float. Some will occur when the float is allowed to run through totally unchecked and actually preceding the bait. Holding back steadily, however, will encourage the bait to fish almost directly beneath the float, thus instantly indicating the tiniest of bites from the wiliest big roach or dace. Those who trot using a centre-pin reel and brake the line by applying gentle thumb pressure to the reels drum, enjoy superb control for easing a stick float downstream. There is in fact no finer reel to use for this technique.

## Finding big roach 22

To locate big roach in our smaller, ri
rivers, walk the river at dawn and
at dusk with binoculars. Big roach
porpoise on the surface, especially o
those frosty mornings, instantly gi
away the whereabouts of the shoa
which tend to occupy the same, ev
paced runs and glides all winter th
Seeing that large, red dorsal fin, fo
by a red tail as the roach rolls is a
and quite unmistakable sight.

Including
John Wilson -
The Early Days
The Exclusive Series
online
FISHING.TV
Welcome To The Home Of Angling Television
263
Programmes To Watch Now
JOIN TODAY!
At last a television channel
just for anglers...
...SPECIAL PROMOTION...SPECIAL PROMOTION...
£40 worth of Ultima line
FREE when you buy a
six month Season Ticket!
SEASON TICKET
SIX MONTHS VIEWING
Choose from our Coarse, Carp,
Sea or Game packs
A six month Season Ticket is just £29.70!!
Come and see for yourself at:
www.onlinefishing.tv
(Promotional offer applies for limited period only)

Le Bounty
Near Le Mans, France
Carp & Cat Fishing
At Its Best
More Than
Just Fishing
Two Well
Stocked Lakes
Bounty 1 Up to 8 Anglers
Bounty 2 Up to 5 Anglers
Excellent Food Package
Superb Showers & Toilets
Fully Licensed Bar
Restaurant
3 Bedroom Mobile Home
fitted out to a high standard
on B2 with its own double swim
0800 849 7091
All booking for Le Bounty are handled by Carpbookings
www.bountylemans.com

Nile Perch Fishing
Lake Nasser Egypt
The African Angler
www.african-angler.net
Email: enquiries@african-angler.net
Tel: + 20 97 2307320

Freshwater Species

# Rudd & Golden Orfe

## Finding rudd 222

Most anglers tend to associate catching rudd with offering free-falling baits close to the surface during the summer months. However, in shallow lakes averaging 3-6 feet, which tend to warm up quickly during mild winter spells, rudd, and large rudd at that, are a very targetable species.

## Winter rudd 223

For winter rudd, try at the deepest end of an estate lake and put out a dozen or so tangerine-sized balls of bread-based ground bait at a short to medium casting distance (say 30 to 50 yards out from the dam). Then, using a two-rod ledgering approach (Avon-style rods are ideal for the job), simply ledger thumbnail-sized lumps of fresh white bread flake covering size 10-8 hooks tied direct to a 4lbs reel line.

## Use bobbins 22

For bite indication when ledgering for rudc rely on simple bobbin-type indicators. Whi many bites will give positive lifts or drops of the bobbin, don't be afraid of striking at two-inch movements. Fishing lighter with smaller baits will only attract smaller rudd. And you could be looking at beautiful golden-sided specimens close to or even exceeding 2lbs. So don't settle for less.

## Rudd/bream hybrids 22

Whilst rudd regularly hybridise with roach wherever both species occur, only rarely in England do rudd/ bream hybrids exist (they are common in Southern Ireland). Rudd/bream hybrids are actually a fine, hard-fighting fish, displaying the finer qualities of bo species. They are thick-set with muted, golden-bronz flanks (quite unlike any other fish) and have scales noticeably larger than a true bream. The fins, howeve are red-brown and the lips usually level.

## Fly-rodding for rudd

Catching rudd on the fly rod during the warm summer months, when they cavort regularly on the surface in th pursuit of hatching flies, is a true delight. An 8 or 9 foot 4-weight outfit with floating line and a fine leader taper to just a 2-3lbs tippet is perfect for the job and allows ruc of all sizes to show their sporting value. By their splashes, identify whether fish are sucking down adult insects on th surface or insects emerging from their pupas in the surfac film, and match your artificial accordingly.

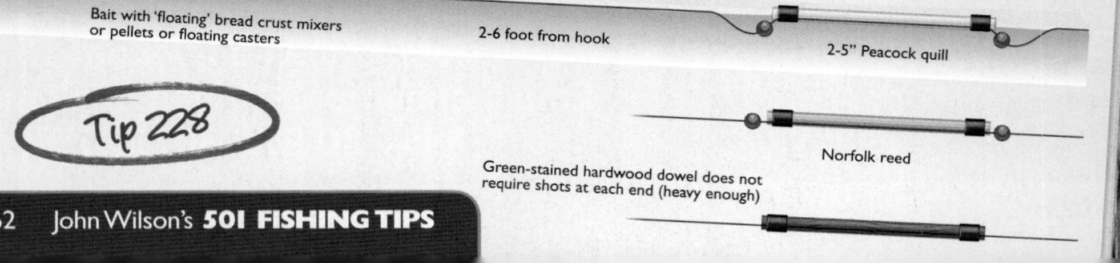

## Tempting with flies 227

Good patterns of dry flies to tempt rudd are black gnat (which represents many adult midges), all the olives and particularly small sedges. They will also move aggressively to lightly leaded imitations presented on the drop such as a mayfly nymph or a shrimp pattern, when nothing is happening on the surface.

## Waggler combo 230

A lightweight, 13-14 foot waggler rod coupled to a baby fixed spool reel filled with clear, 3lbs test mono, is the perfect combo for surface rudd fishing. And you'll need a catapult for regularly putting out floating casters way up wind to get the rudd up on the surface and active.

## Long distances 231

For taking rudd off the top at long distance (30 yards plus), swap the flat-floats for a small tenpin floating controller, stopped by a five turn stop knot and tiny rubber bead, 2-4 foot above the hook. For catching carp/rudd off the top, see Carp Tip 45.

## at floats 228

jeting rudd that are feeding close to or actually from the surface is t effectively practiced using the flat-float controller technique. The roller, which adds both weight for casting in addition to a visual ator, is simply a 2-5 inch length of unpainted peacock quill (what d be more natural floating flat on the surface than a bird quill). mon reed, or (for fishing at greater distances) a third of an inch eter stained hardwood dowel (use green garden fence stain) could ernatives. Each of these three floats is attached to the reel line wide band of silicone rubber at each end, 2-6 foot above the with a shot close up to each end. See diagram opposite.

## Real rudd vs hybrids 232

To distinguish between a true rudd and a roach/rudd hybrid, first look at the fish's lips. The true rudd has a noticeably protruding lower jaw, showing it was purpose built for feeding effectively near the surface, while with hybrids the lips could be level. The body of a true rudd is noticeably deeper than that of either a hybrid or roach, and the colour is of burnished, highly reflective, buttery-gold enamel along the flanks, fusing upwards into olive-bronze along the back. Its fins are bright orange-scarlet, and there is a distinct keel to the anal fin, which is overlapped in a vertical line by the dorsal. Hybrids are of a more even, muted colouration. So if you are in any doubt on any of the above counts about the fish you have just caught, discount it as a true rudd. For rudd/bream hybrids see Tip 225.

## e naturally buoyant baits 229

g a heavier dowel controller, additional casting weight is usually required. But for peacock quill and reed, simply pinch a BB or AA onto the line at each end. Surprising distances can be cast with ontrollers, using naturally buoyant baits like casters, bread crust, lets presented in the surface film. Alternatively, a crust and flake cocktail, or a caster and maggot cocktail can be offered drop. Gloriously positive bites result from fishing the flat float que, with it suddenly sliding across the surface or actually being d under. So hold the rod throughout.

# Rudd & Golden Orfe

## Visit Ireland

233

The numbers of specimen-sized rudd in England (fish between two and three pounds) are becoming less common in England year on year. Ireland, on the other hand, offers superlative rudd fishing in both the north and the south, throughout its canal, river and inter connecting lake-land waterways. Contact Tourism Ireland, 0800 294 2009, or see the feature on p60 & p61.

## Find the shoals

234

In lakes and pits where carp, tench or bream predominate, species at the end of the food chain like rudd, especially big rudd, are at their most catchable when the other species are not. So concentrate on locating the rudd shoals during the middle of the day when they love to bask close to the surface.

## Go large

235

Big rudd also feed in earnest at dusk and dawn, giving away their whereabouts by cavorting and porpoising in the surface film as they inhale emerging insects. They can, however, at such times be encouraged to accept large bottom baits such as a thumbnail-sized piece of bread flake covering a size 8 hook (rudd have large mouths) ledgered over a few handfuls of mashed bread ground bait. But once fish start disappearing from the shoal, sport is often short-lived.

## Ruddy mucus

23

Like roach, rudd are covered in protective mucus which is easily removed by holding them in dry hands. So always wet your han (quickly grabbing the wet landing net mesh will do) before picking one up to unhook.

## Crushed baits 237

Rudd are equipped, as are all cyprinids from gudgeon to the mighty mahseer, with a pair of powerful pharyngeal (throat) teeth for masticating their natural food into a pulp prior to swallowing. This is why worm or maggot baits often come back 'crushed' when you have either missed or not even seen a bite, but your hook must have been sucked back into the fish's throat just the same.

## Missed bites 238

To remedy missed or unregistered bites from rudd, either shorten your hook length if ledgering, or move the bottom shot much closer to the hook if float fishing.

## Free-lining for big rudd 239

For targeting small groups of big rudd which are loath to leave the sanctuary of lily pads during daylight, free lining a slow-sinking bait on the drop often scores where static, bottom-fished baits do not. Try a large piece of fresh white bread flake, lightly pinched onto a size 10 or 8 hook, so that upon landing on the surface it very slowly descends. Experiment in the margins to ascertain exactly how hard you need to pinch the bread on so it sinks slowly, before casting amongst the lilies. And then watch the line like a hawk as the bread slowly sinks, striking instantly into any unusual movement. Fortunately, rudd amongst lilies are invariably bold biters, with the line fair zinging tight or dramatically falling slack, should a fish swim towards the rod.

## Golden Orfe are ruddy similar 240

Golden orfe are not dissimilar to rudd in that they are always on the move, darting about and forever looking upwards in order to intercept falling food items, or one floating on the surface. And everything mentioned in Tips 228, 229 and 230 for catching rudd, will also account for the beautifully coloured golden orfe.

## Golden rudd 241

Golden rudd are quite a rarity in fisheries, although they are a popular pond fish. Their overall salmon-pink colouration is much like the golden orfe, and they are no different to catch than naturally coloured rudd. Because of their bright and distinct colour, they feed quickly when close to the surface. It's almost as though they realise that they are brightly coloured and thus an easy target to predatory birds like the heron and of course pike.

Freshwater Species

# Tench

## 242 Create a channel

To help dour tench fishing come alive, try actually wading into shallow, weedy swims (wearing chest-high waders), and with a long-handled garden rake give the bottom detritus a really good going over whilst creating a wide channel to fish in. In less than an hour's work, a swim can be cleared and the bottom subsequently stirred up with all manner of natural food items left in suspension ready for the tench to turn up in a hungry mood (there is nothing to stop you preparing two or three spots). For deep swims, purchase one of those wide, heavy rake heads to which rope can be tied for throwing out.

## 243 Understanding bubbles

Learning to understand the distinctive feeding bubbles of tench will result in more fish in your net. Small clusters of, say, four to ten small, non-fizzy bubbles rising to the surface come from the fish itself, (through its gills in fact), which is what happens when all cyprinid species masticate their food with their powerful pharyngeal (throat) teeth. Meanwhile, those long lines or patches of larger, fizzy bubbles come from methane trapped immediately below the bottom detritus rising to the surface. You can sometimes actually see bits of twigs and leaves accompanying bubbles into the surface film. This is where a tench, standing on its nose, runs along the bottom to dislodge items of natural food such as shrimps and bloodworms etc.

## 244 Your own bubb

To duplicate the kind o
fizzy bubbles tench se
up via the bottom detri
when feeding aggressive
just run a rod rest or t
end of your landing net
handle along the bottom
of any silty swim. In
particular, try those areas
directly beneath trees and
you will immediately create
the same effect.

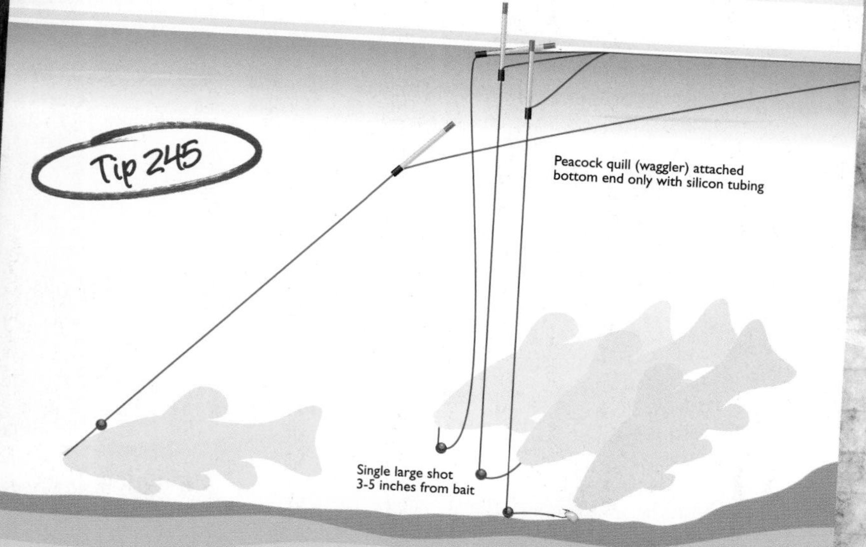


## 245 The lift method

When close-range float fishing, the lift method is phenomenally successful due to the way species like tench feed naturally, by standing on their heads to suck up baits from the bottom. Use a slim stem of buoyant peacock quill (waggler float) attached with silicon tubing at the bottom end only. This not only lifts but actually supports a single large shot fixed on the line 3-5 inches from the bait. During the time it takes the tench to right itself back into to a horizontal position, a firm strike can be made at any time before the float actually lies flat. Once it does, the tench is of course supporting the shot and may eject the bait. So never wait for the float to go under before striking. This applies to all species targeted with the lift-method. See Diagram.

## Male vs female tench 246

Unlike most cyprinids, male and female tench can be told apart easier than any other species. The smaller, often darker, more dogged-fighting males have crinkly, spoon-shaped pelvic fins which, when spread out cover the anal vent, with lumpy, protruding muscles or gonads above. With females, the pelvic fins are smooth, of normal shape and do not cover the vent.

## Quick bobbins 247

For quick and easy attachment of bobbin indicators to your bank sticks when ledgering for tench, simply whip on a tiny rod ring at the top of the bank stick. Then add a snap-link swivel to the end of your bobbin retaining line. Incidentally, a two foot length of 80lbs test Dacron is the perfect material for bobbin retaining lines. Possessing minimal stretch, it will not twang back like heavy monofilament on the strike.

## Baiting in weeds 248

In summer lakes with a covering of filamentous weed on the bottom, tench really respond to ledgered baits that are popped-up just above the weed and in plain view. Try baiting with a large lobworm and inject a little air into the head end, fixing a large shot on the line several inches from the worm so it floats up just above the weed in an attractive, gyrating manner. Alternatively, try a cube of luncheon meat on a hair, to which a piece of buoyant rig foam has been added. Make sure this is threaded on last so it floats uppermost.

## Hook length 249

If when ledgering for tench using small hooks and maggots, the latter come back crushed (indicating they have in fact been sucked back to the fish's pharyngeal teeth for mastication), keep reducing your hook length until hittable bites are registered on your indicator. Alternatively, keep your eyes glued to the line where it goes into the water immediately in front of the rod tip, and strike at any lift or twitch, no matter how slight.

Freshwater Species

# Tench

## Counter subsurface tow 250

Simply pinch one or two 2 or 3x SSG shots onto the retaining line immediately below the bobbin to counteract subsurface tow when ledgering for tench, using bobbin-type indicators such as the tenpin.

## Recognising golden tench 252

There is no favourite or best method for coming to grips with the rare golden tench. This beautiful creature, with a black eye is often called banana fish due to its bright yellowy, sometimes orangey body, flecked all over with small black markings. Golden tench do not tend to hybridise with the common green tench, and exist in only a few isolated fisheries within the British Isles.

## UK golden tenc 25

If you wish to specifically target a rare golden tenc then visit the complex of lakes at the Anglers Paradise fishery in Devon, which contain good numbers of this breath-taking species to 7lbs plus

## Tench at night 251

Wherever clear water tench are unbelievably spooky during the hours of daylight, try float fishing at night using a luminous chemical-element tip sleeved onto a waggler-style float via a piece of clear tubing. Bites not only happen, as the light starts to fade, but are most positive. The lift-method works well here. See Tip 245.

## Tench in reeds 254

When casting tight up to reed lines from the bank or an anchored punt or boat, use a bodied waggler float rig with most of the bulk shot grouped around the base (which precedes the bait during the cast). Have just two small shots down the line, the lowest 6-8 inches from the hook coming to rest on the bottom once the bait has arced downwards through the water to settle immediately below the float, mere inches from the reed stems along which tench patrol.

## Taking summer tench 255

Ledgering method-feeder-style is a deadly way of taking summer tench, especially from distant swims. Use a ground bait mix that breaks down quickly (it's no good lying there clogged around the frame feeder for 30 minutes when tench are on the rampage) and use a short 4-6 inch hook length. Include hook bait samples like casters, chopped worm, corn or small feed pellets in your ground bait mix, whilst baiting with the same on the hook.

## Soft hook pellets 256

To complement a pellet-based feeder ground bait, soft hook pellets are especially effective whether hair rigged or side hooked. Alternatively, and this works great over filamentous bottom weed, hair rig artificial floating sweet corn, which floats up above the weed. Tench hit it like it's the only kernel of corn left in the lake. Artificial casters can score too.

## Forget hair-rigging and bolt rigs 257

Free-lining for tench may well seem an ancient technique in these days of hair-rigging and bolt rigs, but in certain situations it can still produce. Tench hugging the margins amongst reed mace or sedges, for instance, are likely to flee when a heavy bolt-lead rig is sploshed in amongst them. Also, you can easily cast for tench moving through gaps in dense weed immediately below the rod tip, or simply tench moving very close in through clear water.

## Free line baits 258

In each of the above situations, free-lined bait is liable to be immediately inhaled without suspicion. Or you could try a large piece of soft protein paste, a piece of slow-sinking bread flake or, better still, a bait of balanced paste and crust that will come to rest on top of the most dense weed.

## Free-lining essentials 259

To free line effectively, you need to be nicely camouflaged and kneeling or sitting well back from the water's edge so that only the end of your rod hangs out over the surface along the margins. You then simply watch the fish or the line between surface and rod tip for bites, and you'll enjoy the most glorious of uninhibited slow indications, where you can almost pre-empt the line lifting and snaking out behind the tench as it moves away with your bait, before striking firmly. And what fights and long runs you'll enjoy as a consequence! So use an Avon-type rod and just a 6lbs reel line with a number 6 hook tied direct.

## Use those fingers 260

When immediate bites are expected to a free-lined bait, simply hook your forefinger around the line just above the bale arm, so that you'll still feel the line move should your attentions be elsewhere.

## Angled rods 261

For long free-lining sessions, rig up both front and rear rod rests with the rod tip angled downwards, and loop a coil of silver kitchen foil around the line between reel and butt ring on a two foot drop. Fish with a closed bale arm so you can strike the instant the foil indicator either rises or drops back.

Freshwater Species

# Trout

## Bring out the Czech nymphs
262

When sight-casting to monster rainbows and big browns of small, clear-watered, man-made lakes often won't play ball, so try this. Closely observe the movement route of the particular trout you're after (most big, small-water trout adopt a favoured feeding route) and select an area where it usually comes close. Now, with your prize trout well out of sight, roll out a heavily weighted Czech nymph of a colour you can clearly see, tied to a long leader and allow it to free fall down to the bottom at a spot over which the trout will eventually pass. Keep your eyes glued to the exact spot and when the fish next comes round, twitch your Czech nymph up off the bottom clearly within its path.

## Float tubing
263

For an entirely different slant on modern fly fishing for trout, why not try float-tubing? Many lake-land and reservoir trout fishery complexes up and down the country encourage this fascinating approach and even have equipment for hire. If you already own a set of diving fins and lightweight, chest-high waders however, you may even wish to purchase your own tube.

## The tube
264

To enjoy a day's tubing, simply walk backwards into the water (fins/flippers already on) with shoulder straps supporting the tube which has an open front, across which is stretched a webbing seat, and suddenly you're afloat. Most purpose-built tubes have zipped compartments on top to house necessities, and can be easily inflated (built-in tubes for blowing into) and deflated in minutes. You get to explore all those awkward-to-fis tree-covered spots around islands, and there is a wonderful sense of freedom when out tubing. And subsequently playing fis when actually in the water is pure joy.

## All-year-round trout
265

Fancy some action with jet propelled rainbows and maybe even the occasional big brown during the cold winter months? It's fabulous fun! Gone are the days when fly fishers packed away their rods throughout the winter because trout were perpetuating their spawning cycle. Today, progressive still-water fisheries stock only with triploids, with trout coming from eggs that have been subjected to a heat-shock treatment, making them sexless adults. These remain in tip-top silver condition all year round, and fighting fit, using all their energy packing on weight as opposed to producing eggs or milt.

## Up for a fight? 266

And how do triploids fight in cold water conditions? If anything, they actually battle harder and for considerably longer during the winter, particularly in deep, clear, still water fisheries. So what's stopping you?

## Imitation flies 267

Though individually small in size, the family of midges which we fly fishermen refer to as buzzers (because the hordes of egg-carrying females when gyrating over the water at head height audibly buzz), includes more than 400 species, and is easily the most important family of flies for the still-water angler. But really, all the fly fisherman needs to fool most trout is a couple of imitations, say black and red standard buzzer patterns, and the same again in suspender or emerger versions, where flotation fibres at their heads suspend them in the surface film, with their bodies hanging vertically.

## uable midge larva 268

midge larva, non other than the bloodworm, is arguably one of the most fic and thus the most valuable sources of natural food not only for trout, or all our cyprinid species, from rudd to the largest carp.

## orget drift fishing 269

hen boat fishing huge expanses of still water like eservoirs, and the trout are staying deep due to bright onditions, the standard technique of drift fishing does not always work. This is because by the time you have cast out and let the team of flies sink to the right depth before starting the retrieve, the cast is almost back to the boat and you have to recast. Far better therefore to anchor-up and let the flies sink to the required depth, then make the retrieve at your own pace.

## Barometric pressure 270

Barometric pressure is something we all know must seriously affect our sport, but rarely get to pin point when. Those who regularly fish small, man-made, clear water trout fisheries where trout can be clearly seen repeatedly refusing whatever fly is put before them, have noticed that the trout's mood changes drastically in line with a change in barometric pressure. Here they suddenly snap at anything for a few casts, before going back to being difficult again. And those whose wrist watch shows that pressure change, have subsequently bagged up. Food for thought, eh?

# Trout

## Success with cold water trout 271

For catching cold water trout in the early spring which are stocked into the deep water of reservoirs and gravel-pit fisheries, then presenting a booby fished on a short 3-5 foot leader and Hi-D, ultra fast sinking line is one hell of an effective way of turning a hopeless' day into success.

## Boobies 272

Boobies are so effective because they work in reverse to all other flies. When you start to retrieve, having allowed enough time for much of your Hi-D line to be laying on the bottom, boobies tied around the hook, will angle sharply downwards as opposed to upwards like all other artificials. So even the most wily and fished-for trout won't have the slightest reservation in gobbling them up. Most fish are in fact hooked way back in the throat.

## The priest 273

If purchasing your first priest for dispatching your catch quickly, then select one where one end unscrews and reverses to become a marrow spoon. This, when sleeved down the trout's throat and into the top of its stomach, will, after pressing its belly gently, tell you exactly what insects it has been feeding upon, so that you can match your artificial to the natural.

## Buy a smoker 27

To obtain the utmost enjoyment from catching trout, particularly large rainbows, invest in a specialised smoker. Via a small methylated spirit burner heating hardwood, aromatic sawdust placed on top of the heating plate, this equipment cures, cooks and hot smokes your catch all in one. Try putting the hot-smoked flank of a large trout, wrapped in silver foil together with a large knob of butter and masses of coarse-ground black pepper, onto the Bar-B-Q. Lovely!

## Essentials 2

When casting a fly, alwa wear a hat, preferably o with a peak to alleviate g and concentrate your fie of vision (shield your eye with your hand as if look into the sun and you will see what I mean) plus Polarised glasses. Togethe they greatly reduce the painful experience of a fly, travelling over 50 miles a hour, embedding in your head, or worse still, an eye

## 276 Categorise your flies

If fly fishing from the bank, spread your fly collection around your waistcoat in a number of small boxes, each holding different patterns such as nymphs, lures, dry flies, emergers, buzzers, and so on, as opposed to one large (wooden) box. Upon leaving the car, you can then set off with exactly the types and patterns of flies that might be required during your day's fishing, instead of carting the kitchen sink around.

## 277 Trout love mayfly time

Endeavour, even if it's only once in your lifetime, to be beside a top chalk stream trout fishery with rod in hand, at mayfly time. The thickest hatches of this extraordinary aquatic insect usually occur during the last couple of weeks in May, and trout gorge themselves silly. After getting your hand in with two or three easy fish, you'll know whether trout are showing a preference for the newly-hatched fly or spent insects lying on the surface, inert with their wings stretched out. You can then take time in stalking one of those whopper brown trout that only ever seem to present any chance of them sucking down an artificial, during the mayfly cycle.

## 278 ouble-haul casting

or fly fishing all day, without the undue fatigue of ontinually bringing your rod back and forwards in rder to get a long line out, learn the art of double-haul asting. This entails roll casting, say, a third of your line orwards, (following the retrieve) and momentarily pulling ıard on the line during the back cast to accelerate its flight. A second downwards pull or haul is then made (with your hand gripping the line immediately below the butt ring) prior to making the forward cast. And this acceleration will shoot out whatever line you have on the ground. It is in fact easier to do than explain because it's mostly all down to feel and timing. But turning round to watch the flight of your back cast will help enormously. And remember that the line must be as straight in the air as possible at the beginning of each haul, whether forwards or backwards.

## 279 now your trout

oth golden and blue rainbow trout are not different ecies, merely coloured variants of the rainbow trout, hereas, a brown bow is a sterile hybrid resulting rom the crossing of a rainbow with a brown trout. he cheetah is another sterile hybrid, resulting from he crossing of a rainbow with an American brook trout. And the tiger is a sterile hybrid resulting from the crossing of an American brook trout with a brown trout. Nowadays, these colourful trout are stocked only into a handful of southern chalk-stream fed lakes.

## 280 Don't forget drogues when fly fishing

Never set out across a trout reservoir for a day's fly fishing without a drogue. This is employed in windy conditions to slow down the boat's drift so that you have more control over the way your flies are fishing. See On the Drift and Trolling Tip 342.

## 281 Drifting loch-style

One of the most delightful ways of catching reservoir trout is to drift loch style, casting ahead of the drifting boat set sideways-on to the wind (with a drogue over the windward side) into the relatively calm surface of wind lanes. Long casts are generally made down a particular lane, and a team of three flies steadily retrieved back to the boat. Watch out for rainbows especially, which appear from nowhere, just as you start the backwards cast, to shoot up and grab the point fly or sometimes even the bob.

# Salmon & Sea Trout

## 282 Use a heavy-weighted nymph

Fancy catching a salmon on a 5 or 6 weight trout, brook-rod, and a leader tapered to just 6lbs test? Well, it is certainly not impossible. You just need a little confidence, and access to smallish clear-flowing rivers where salmon are known to rest up fairly close into the bank, because casting is not in any order of importance here. Having identified a lie close into the bank, immediately downstream from a croy, or beside pilings or behind a salmon stone, the secret is to let a really heavily weighted nymph (a gold head for instance) quickly reach bottom following a short roll cast made square on. Lift it steadily upwards to the surface, where, every so often, a salmon, having followed it up through sheer curiosity, will nail it just before, or actually on the top. Sounds strange I know, but the technique really works well on small rivers, particularly southern chalk streams.

## Work out patrol routes 283

Selecting the right artificial to tempt Atlantic salmon is almost an impossibility. These particular oddities do seem to feed on natural food items, and strangely, do not colo up as might be expected, even when still uncaught in a lake for a year or more. A trait they do follow, however, is that even in large lakes they seem to favour definite patr routes, which take them close into the bank, similar to th characteristics of large brown trout. So it's not so much t fly offered, but where and at what depth.

## Using spoons 284

When using Toby-type spoons for catching salmon, a multiplier outfit (6 or 7001 sized left-hand wind) not only fits snugly into your hand (go for a trigger-grip reel fitting, behind which your forefinger sits comfortably), but counting the lure down to the river be before clicking the reel back into gear is so much easier than with a fixed spool reel. Start by casting directly across the flow and once the spoon touches bottom, simply put the reel back into gear and, holding the rod tip up, allow the current to bounce and wobble the spoon slowly across the rive occasionally touching bottom. Do not attempt to retrieve as the spoon comes around or it will rise and work too fast for a salmon to grab hold. It pays to have several different weights (from say 12 to 28, even 40 grams) of the same colour spoon amongst your kit, to work varying depths and current speeds.

## The downstream lure 285

When the lure reaches the end of its downstream arc and starts to dangle just like a fly, then, and only then, start a slow retrieve. When the spoon is back at the rod, take a short pace downstream and repeat the cast. In wide rivers make two casts at each spot before moving. The first short and the second long, to cover all potential lies.

## Devon minnow 286

One of the most famous salmon and sea trout lures, the Devon minnow can really produce in cold water conditions. It is offered in the traditional, 'downstream and across' technique with a banana-shaped Wye lead built into the trace 3 feet above the lure, which bounces over a rocky bottom. Alternatively, it is presented on a separate 3 foot link joined to a three way swivel, below which is a 1-2 foot mono link and bomb, or stick weight that literally bounce over the river bed. A buoyant, balsa wood Devon will then spin well above any snags. It's always worth keeping a few different patterns in your waistcoat.

## When in Sweden... 287

In Sweden, a similar rig to the latter method is used in conjunction not with lures, but large tube flies. It catches plenty of sea trout and salmon too.

## Long trotting 289

During the summer and autumn, long trotting for salmon in many of our smaller rivers, using a centre-pin reel and a preserved shrimp presented attractively beneath a wide-topped float, will account for fish holding station in awkward, weedy, even impossible lies. Rig up an Avon-style rod with an 8-10lbs test reel line and a chubber float carrying 4-5 SSG shots. Bulk this 18 inches above a size 8 treble hook with a 1½-2 inch shrimping pin threaded onto the line in between, so that it can be sleeved through the bait to keep it straight before nicking the treble into the head.

## e Flying C 288

.over runs or pools that can only be roached from downstream, one lure s all others. So don't go salmon or trout fishing anywhere without a few ng Condoms in your kit. Referred nore reverently as the Flying C, this n elongated Mepp's-type spinner a long, heavy shaft and treble k, over which is sleeved a coloured ber tube. This lure is at its most ective when cast directly upstream l across. After touching bottom, it is n retrieved downstream and across h the flow. It's a technique that gives th salmon and sea trout a much orter period of indecision, due to the gle and reduced length of time at ich the lure cuts across their field of ion. And for this reason, the Flying can prove deadly.

## Pretty shrimps 290

To present the preserved shrimp attractively, set the float to work the bait 1-2 feet above the river bed, and trot through at current pace, holding back on the float every so often so the bait rises up attractively. Expect bold bites, as though you were trotting for chub.

## The needle knot 291

For joining a full line or a shooting head to braided backing, use either the Albright knot (see Tip 351) or the standard needle knot. See diagram.

## At night 292

here is no doubt, especially in low and clear water conditions, that fly fishing or sea trout throughout the hours of darkness vastly improves your chances of ooking up. But even shallow, intimate little rivers take on an entirely different haracter at night. So before you set forth into the night, walk your river slowly luring daylight taking account of where trees and bushes are situated along ach of the pools you intend covering and actually wade in to roughly where you vill stand to cast. Take a good look all around on the bottom for large boulders r tree stumps that might trip you up and work out your casting angles equired to move steadily along the pool, taking into account that fish will often ot be so far away under the cloak of darkness.

# Salmon & Sea Trout

## 293 Prepare for night angling

When tackling sea trout at night, be certain that everything you might need, from a small torch to a pair of scissors, spare tippet material to a small pair of forceps, plus your fly boxes are all stored and easily reachable within the pockets of your waistcoat or wading vest. Realising that your favourite flies are in a tackle bag back in the car when half way down a promising pool in the pitch black, is no laughing matter.

## 294 Using a heavy wading staff

When tackling big, fast and boulder-strewn rivers for salmon or sea trout, wading up past your waistline, it is imperative to work yourself into a casting position for covering some pools. Do not leave the bank without a heavy wading staff, that is retained around your shoulders on a lanyard. You can then feel your way downriver.

## 29 Quality waders

A pair of good quality, breathable, or neoprene chest high waders is an indispensable piece of kit to all salmon and sea trout fisherman, whether they Spey cast or throw artificial lures. To alleviate slipping algae-covered stones and rocks ar risk a ducking in freezing cold wat wading boots, which are worn over the integral neoprene socks, shoulc have felt soles, as should waders with integral rubber boots. For rea cold spring conditions, all-neopren waders 5-6mm thick with integral, felt-soled boots are recommended

## 29 Spey casting

One important thing to remember about Spey casting is always allow the bow in the D to fully form and hang bes you, before roll-casting the fly out. It's then so easy.

## 297 Catch bigger

Here's a handy tip that I picked up at the famous junction beat on Scotland's River Tweed when Spey casting for salmon. Cast downstream and across and roll an upstream loop in the line to mend it, whilst holding the rod parallel with and low to the water as the line swings round. Then try moving the rod back, say, nine or ten inches, every few seconds, which moves the fly attractively at the other end in short surges. It induces takes on days when the fish are not really having it. Try it and see.

## Make use of river conditions 298

Remember that the exact height of a river will have a great influence on the chances of catching, whether fly fishing or working artificials. Ideally, a steadily falling river with the water clearing after a flood is most likely to induce salmon to lie-up in the pools for longer periods. Moreover, with the previous occupants nearly all having migrated upstream during the last spate, most fish in each pool will be newcomers and likely to hit the first angler's offering they see.

## Worming or prawn fishing 299

Worming or prawn fishing for salmon works when other methods do not, particularly in difficult times like when the river is heavily coloured and out of sorts. Do not be put off by the stigma that some game fishermen like to attach to bait fishing. A salmon does not fight any the less for being hooked on bait. It's down to how you value that fight.

## Letting them off the hook 300

In these days of diminishing salmon returns from most river systems within the British Isles, should you not wish to eat your catch, do not even attempt to net or especially, handle it. Using a pair of long-nosed artery forceps, slip the hook free whilst it is lying beaten on its side, and take great pleasure in watching it swim off.

## Knowing your species 301

To work out whether you have caught a salmon or a sea trout, or indeed a giant brown trout, grip firmly around its tail root. Salmon have a narrow tail root often referred to as a wrist, with a ridged and distinct keel to their tail and so can easily be lifted up. Brown and sea trout, on the other hand, have soft tail edges against which your hand will slip. So they cannot be easily lifted.

# Zander

## Use bobbin indicators 302

Zander are arguably, more sensitive to resistance, than any other British freshwater species. So when ledgering live or dead baits, opt for a lightweight bobbin indicator (that clips onto the line between reel and butt ring) hung on a two foot drop. This is much better than drop-off indicators, which require significantly more pressure on behalf of the fish to register an indication. There are days when this makes all the difference between runs developing, and the bait being repeatedly dropped.

## Try the Drachkovitch rig 303

Even in heavily coloured water with mere inches of visibility you can enjoy hectic sport with zander. Their large, light-reflecting eyes are purpose built for hunting in low light conditions when the eyes of their prey, such as small roach, rudd, dace and bleak, are not. Try working a 3-5 inch freshly killed bleak up and down 'sink and draw' style, close to the bottom mounted on a double treble trace. The most successful of all rigs is the Drachkovitch rig invented by Frenchman Albert Drachkovitch. This comprises a lightweight V-shaped sprung wire stem inserted down the dead bait's throat, to which at the top clip is attached a ball weight of between (depending upon depth, casting distance and current force) 4-12 grams. Also attached to the clip is around six inches of stiff copper wire, which is threaded once through the bleak's slim body at the shoulder, and then wound firmly around the body. Two single trebles joined to wire or tough braid, one short and one long, are pushed into the fish's flank and tail root on opposing sides, to ensure a hook-up from whatever angle the zander grabs hold. Expect those juddery, snappy takes from zander both on th drop, as the bait flutters, and whilst on the jerk, by working the bait constantly with your rod tip. Strike at anything positive.

## High season for zander 30

Q: When is the best time to go zander fish in the British Isles? A: Following a couple weeks of intermittent, often, heavy rain, the rivers are well up and running the colour of strong tea. This enigmatic predator, with its huge glassy eyes, is superbly equipped for hunting out its preferred prey of small shoal fishes like roach, rudd, dace, gudgeo bleak and skimmer bream, both during the hours of darkness and when flooded river offer minimal visibility. Exactly the kind of conditions you would not fancy for pike fis are exactly what zander prefer.

## At night
**305**

During the warmer months, dusk and dawn are prime times for finding zander in a feeding mood. And of course, at any time during the hours of darkness, especially during mild spells of winter weather.

## Strike fast
**306**

Whether you offer lures or use dead or live baits to tempt zander, you will catch infinitely more fish by striking instantly, certainly earlier rather than later. Since this predator is ultra-sensitive to resistance, the worst course of action is to allow several yards of line to evaporate from the spool, as you would prior to hitting a run from other predators such as eels, pike and catfish. The further it runs off with your bait, the more resistance it will feel, especially if it runs off at right angles to the ledger bomb (zander living in Fenland Drains have no option but to run along the drain) and eventually it will either eject the bait, or you will be unable to straighten the line out in order to set the hooks.

## Get twitching
**307**

Twitching a small dead bait back just above bottom after waiting some time without a run, is often the trigger to catching this finicky feeder. So above your wire trace and two-treble hook set-up, with a large bead on the reel line in between, use a bomb link-ledger, which ensures the bait won't foul bottom during the twitch back. Eight inches of stiff rig tubing is threaded over 15lbs mono to form the link, with a bomb tied at one end and a ¼inch diameter ring and buoyant rig foam body at the top. This set-up can be used in conjunction with a ledger bobbin, and the bait left static for a minute or two between bouts of twitching. It will certainly keep you active alternating between two or three rods.

## Zander love fresh kills
**308**

To catch zander on small live and dead baits choose roach, rudd or dace (gudgeon work well too) between 3 and 5 inches long. Every so often, a big zander will wolf down an 8 inch skimmer bream intended for pike, as they will the occasional sea dead bait, like a smelt or a herring. But generally speaking, zander are not receptive to sea baits, nor anything over large. What they do seem to home into, however, and often with surprising speed, are small, indigenous, freshwater fish freshly killed that have been stabbed a few times with a sharp knife, immediately prior to casting, which allows those attractive juices to permeate quickly downstream with the current. Try it and see.

## US zander
**309**

While there is just the one species called zander in European rivers and lakes, two extremely similar species, sauger, and the larger, walleye, are found in North American freshwater. A small number of North American walleye were in fact introduced into The Fens way back in 1925, long before the controversial stock of 97 zander were introduced into the Great Ouse Relief Channel in 1963.

## UK record
**310**

There is actually a British record walleye that weighed 11lb 12oz, caught from the River Delph by Mr F Adams in 1934. However, European zander were being brought across the Channel by boat to stock The Duke of Bedford's Lakes at Woburn as early as the 1870s,. And there were numerous subsequent stockings of both European and home-grown zander into various southern waters during the 1920s, 1940s and 1950s.

## Drag and resistance
**311**

You'll catch far more zander, and enjoy their scrap much more, by using the different tackle to that used for pike. And it's all down to reducing drag and resistance to a biting fish. An 8lbs reel line matched to an Avon-type rod, for instance, is quite adequate or 10lbs test at the most (double figure barbel come out on the same strength, and such fish fight far harder than zander).

Freshwater Species

# Zander

## Trace wire and hooks 312

A soft, fine, multi-strand wire of around 15lb test twisted onto a size 10 swivel, is more than adequate, yet strong enough for pike should one pick up your bait intended for zander. And with hooks, a duo of semi-barbed fine wire, size 10, fits the bill admirably.

## Short lifts and drops 315

Learn to pull into mere one and two inch lifts or drops of the ledger bobbin when ledgering with small dead baits in clear water conditions, and when zander are being particularly finicky. Sometimes, any stronger indications simply will not happen before the bait is ejected.

## Eel or lamprey 316

Short, two to three inch sections of ½ - ¾ inch diameter eel or lamprey ledgered static on the bottom can prove magical. At such times, zander will show a complete and distinct preference for them to all other dead baits.

## Avoiding twists 313

If ledgering small live or dead baits for zander, and the mono bomb link that slides on the line above your wire trace repeatedly twists around the wire, then here's how to alleviate the problem. First, make the 4-6 inch bomb link from stiff 20lbs test mono. And second, incorporate a 10 inch section of mono (same as reel line) above your wire trace, the top swivel of which (with a bead in between) the swivel of your bomb link rests against. Tangles will then not happen.

## Easy does it 314

When striking into zander be gentle. Simply wind down to take up any slack and slowly pull the rod back and upwards whilst reeling. Most times the hooks actually find purchase when the zander opens its mouth and shakes its head from side to side in order to eject the bait, just like a perch. And a heavy strike at this time will only pull out the trebles, especially from lightly hooked fish.

## Zander hotspots

**317**

In rivers and slow-moving drains, trotting live bait downstream beneath a sliding float rig, into areas of low light such as beneath road and rail bridges, can really prove productive. Such areas are inevitably quite deep and are usually prime zander hotspots. So plumb each run accurately and set the float to present the bait (a gudgeon or small roach) two feet above bottom, with a swan shot pinched onto the wire trace just below the swivel to keep it down, and wind quickly down to pull into a fish immediately the float disappears. Wait too long and it will feel resistance and eject the bait.

## Rubber shads

**318**

On some of our larger rivers where zander have become well established, such as the River Severn, the Warwickshire Avon or the River Nene, locating them using a fish finder can provide superlative daytime sport with artificial lures, particularly rubber shads. Generally, the smaller sizes are best, when worked in a jigging, up and down action once bottom has been found.

## Try Storm artificials

**319**

By far the best selection of synthetic rubber shad-like artificials is marketed through Storm. Available in just about every shape size and colour, many of these decidedly 'real to the touch' soft rubber and plastic, internally-leaded artificials are fitted with just a large single hook protruding from behind the dorsal fin. These models are ideal for working in and around weedy and snaggy areas without catching up.

## Elaborate lures

**320**

Some rubber and plastic bodied lures come fitted with a small treble protruding from the pelvic fins. These really attract and catch zander due to the vibratory, throbbing action from either curl or block tails. Some even have holographic flash foil, scented bodies impregnated with various oils. All have life-like swimming actions, and some are actually designed to be trolled. Try them all. But stick to the smaller zander-sized models of between 9-14cm in length.

## The ultimate combination

**321**

An ideal combo for working rubbers is an 8-9 foot, tip-actioned spinning rod coupled to a small fixed spool reel or baby multiplier, loaded with 12-18lbs test braid. Hits are often extremely gentle taps and judders of the rod tip, and you need to strike into any potential hit, no matter how slight the pull. Where pike are regularly encountered, a short (5-6 inch) but soft, multi-strand wire trace is imperative.

2

# Going the DISTANCE

- At Anchor
- On the Drift and Trolling

**"Don't be afraid to go out on a limb. That's where the fruit is."**

## Freshwater Boat Fishing

# At Anchor

### Use heavy mud weights 322

There is nothing more frustrating than when the boat suddenly drifts away and out of the action because your mud weights have lifted. Even moreso, when runs from pike are coming thick and fast, or the swim fills up with feeding bream or tench. So invest in the best and heaviest pair of mud weights that you can lift, and shackle them (visit a boat chandler) to soft, half-inch thick rope, at least 30 feet in length. Thin ropes cut into your fingers all too easily. I also carry along a third weight for extra stability in extreme winds and currents, which is lowered over one side amidships.

### The best of the best 323

The 30-50lbs steel weights fitted to cruisers are the best mud weights money can buy. Being small for their weight they are easily transportable. Mud or silt, which clings to the bottom with surprising ease, is easily shaken off before bringing them onboard by swishing from side to side (imperative when moving swims). And since you will hopefully only ever purchase one pair, while expensive, they are money well spent.

### Economy weights 3

To economise on mud weights, fill a couple of 2-3 gallon plastic buckets with cement. This provides a couple of cheap (boat-friendly) mud weights, which benefit from already being covered in plastic. Remember to make a couple of sm holes two inches apart in the top of each bucket-to take a U of ¼ inch diameter mild steel rod, for tying th rope to. And lay the bucket on its bottom (with two inches of your U of steel rod in the ground, with the ends bent back inside the bucket) before filling with a strong mix. Remember to smooth the cement over thoroughly when level with the lip of each bucket. Mud clings with ease to a rough surface.

### Train tracks 325

If you know of anyone on the railways, old steel railway track cut into 12 inch lengths, makes for formidable mud weights, and is easy to tie on.

### Point upstream, not sideways 32

When anchoring in deep and fast-flowing water, such as t tidal reaches of my local rivers which feed the Norfolk Br for instance, do not plan to anchor sideways on to the flow It is far better to put the bows of the boat pointing directly upstream before lowering down your first mud weight on long rope, at least twice that of river depth. Three times fo extreme conditions. Then once the boat has come to settle directly down river, lower your second weight over the tra on a short rope. This should keep the boat as steady as it ever going to be in a current. A third weight put down at amidships will reduce any sideways yawing to a minimum.

### Oars and rowlocks 327

When purchasing oars, it is well worthwhile investing in a quality pair of exactly the correct length for your boat and installing a pair of rowlocks which actually fit the protective rubber collar on the oars. There is nothing more frustrating - embarrassing even - should you tip over backwards within sight of other boats due to the oars pulling out of over-size rowlocks when leaning back into the rowing against a headwind.

### Empty your boat 32

Remember NOT to keep your oars on the boat if it is tied to a permanent mooring. Get into the habit of taking them home along with your engine and petrol tank.

## Anchored carp fishing 329

Do you know that carp fishing from an anchored boat (in either river or lake) is not only possible but, where few other anglers ever bother to go afloat, sport can actually prove surprisingly good. Put down a carpet of maize or wheat-based particle feed a few days prior to fishing (which includes major attractors like well-stewed hempseed and tares or tic beans) and add some hook baits like chopped up boilies and halibut pellets. This can only improve results (don't forget to mark the spot with an empty plastic bottle on a cord tied to a house brick), which largely depend on being able to anchor your boat really steadily. Almost a technique in itself!

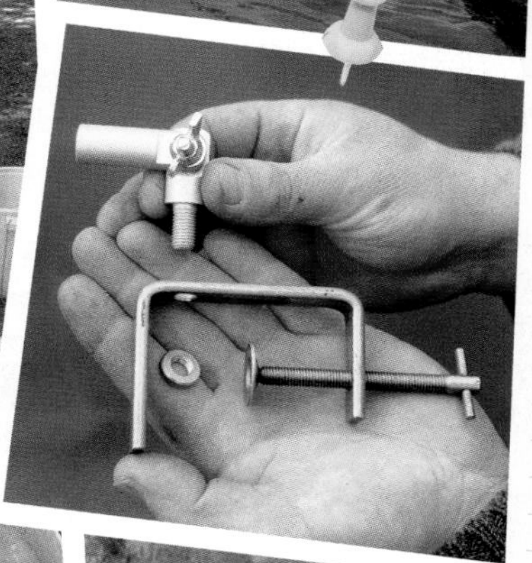

## Tying on weights 330

Flat-bottomed craft like aluminium boats with semi-flat hulls are best, and wobble about the least, providing a wonderfully stable platform. However, whatever your craft, the secret to carp fishing from a boat is having three really heavy mud weights (each of at least 50-60lbs apiece) with two of them tied to long ropes. And by long I mean at least five times swim depth. For fishing in rivers, put the bows of the boat into the flow and drop the front weight, paying out all the rope. Tie it off around a cleat and drop the stern mud weight. Now start pulling the boat back upstream on the bows rope while paying out rope at the stern. When you have equal lengths of rope in the boat, which means you are anchored mid-way between the two weights, tie off both ends really tightly. Then put down your third weight amidships and tie off.

## ake a gunwhale bracket 331

 now have the steadiest floating platform possible in both still and nning water (it is the same process for anchoring in lakes and pits) m which bolt-rig ledgering becomes immensely enjoyable, using reel's free-spool facility as your bite indicator, for carp or tench hing. It's great for float fishing too. Try it and see. This way of choring was introduced to me by top angling guide Gary Allen o takes visitors after big carp and catfish along prolific stretches the Rivers Segre and Ebro at Mequinenza in north eastern pain. Contact Gary via: garyallenfishing@gmail.com or visit ww.garyallensregencyangling.com. Alternatively, call: 0034 667 55863. Whilst commercially produced boat-rod rests are available om specialist tackle shops to suit both trolling and at anchor shing, homemade front rod rests for float fishing and special eep net angle locks for gunwale fixing are easily constructed by ne DIY enthusiast. To make a gunwale bracket, simply drill a 3/8th f an inch hole through the top of a small steel G clamp. This then ccommodates either a front rod rest head of your choice, or the pecial angle top tilt built into top of the range keep nets, allowing the net ring to lie horizontal to the surface. For nets not fitted with this device, simply screw an angle-lock into the G clamp and secure, as with the rod rest top, by a 3/8th BSF nut.

## Organise your equipment 332

Don't wait until you are close to or actually anchored up over your favourite spot before laying out all your equipment within the boat in an organised manner. A quick getaway at the moorings by dumping everything in haphazardly could cost you dearly in lost sport later on due to all the moving and scuffing about. So take time while the boat is still tied up to store everything where it won't slide or bang about. Set up the landing net and position the mud weights at exactly the spots from where they are going to be lowered at the bows and stern. Make up all the rods and rigs required (I take mine along already made up and broken down with elastic bands holding them together at both ends), and store them lengthways inside the boat (banks of 3-6, tubed, vertical American-style rod holders are indispensable for this). Therefore, as you approach the intended fishing area, the boat can be positioned side-on and both mud weights lowered simultaneously with the absolute minimum of noise thereafter. An old piece of carpet underlay laid on the bottom of the boat will help to deaden most of your shuffling about.

Freshwater Boat Fishing

# At Anchor

## Exploring in your boat 333

Boat fishing really does open up a whole new world to fresh water anglers, whether pike fishing remote parts of the Norfolk Broads and their connecting tidal rivers, or tench, bream, or carp fishing amongst the tranquillity of a secluded estate lake, mere, reservoir or gravel pit. You get to explore areas and swims never fished from the shore, and thus fish that have rarely had bait offered to them. And even ledgering can be enjoyed from a boat properly anchored. See Tip 330.

## Other boating options 334

A lightweight but stable (flat bottomed) car-top dinghy will get you started in boat fishing. Alternatively, try a lightweight foldaway one and two-man boat, such as the Samalite Discovery foldaway dinghy and the folding Portabote. And if you really catch the 'get away from it all' bug then it's well worth investing in a pucker 12-14 foot aluminium fishing boat and trailer which can then literally be taken anywhere. Aluminium hulls require absolutely no maintenance and thus hold their price. And they are available with extras such as rod holders, swivel seats and water-tight compartments for stowage, to make life afloat all the more comfortable and enjoyable.

## Take binoculars 33

A good quality pair of binoculars (mine are size 10 x 42, and about the most powerful you can hold steady using one hand) are indispensable when boat fishing. You can see from afar, before getting too close, the feeding bubbles of tench, bream or carp, and thus lower the mud weights long before scaring them. You can see fish swirling on the surface and capitalise by moving to the same spot. You can observe the floats and direction to which other anglers pike fishing the same water are fishing, so a wide berth can be given when on the move. And of course watching our native and migrant birdlife when out afloat adds an enchanting aspect to the world of angling.

## Essential clothing 33

As my experiences of spending close on 40 years pike fishing the windswept and lonely waters of the Norfolk Broads have proved, you should always set out well equipped against the elements when boat fishing at anchor in the depths of winter. Even if it's warm and sunny when you arrive, think twice about leaving the thermal gear in the car. In addition to a good quality waterproof ¾ length coat with a built-in hood (I wear a separate, peaked hat anyway so I don't have to sit on a sunny day forever squinting), wear layers of warm clothing beneath. Don't just settle for waterproof trousers - a tall, salopette-type bib and brace combo with shoulder straps, and long zips down the waterproof trouser leg bottoms are worth their weight in gold. Alternatively, some prefer a one-piece waterproof suit (over a thermal under suit) which certainly keeps all the draughts out. Should the weather turn warm later on in the day, you can always remove your top coat, if wearing separates.

## 337 istant hot food

eryone has their very own favourite food to take boat
shing. And while I guess Pot Noodles are not everyone's
lea of real food, we are talking about something hot and
ourishing here with the least amount of fuss when sitting
n a rocking boat, possibly in the rain or snow miles from
nowhere. So simply taking along a flask of boiling hot
water for adding to instant meals like Pot Noodles (you
get enough water for at least three pots from the average
flask) plus some crunchy, pre-buttered rolls for dunking
requires little forethought. They are far more warming
than cheese sandwiches!

## 338 iding huddled baits

is nothing worse than going afloat pike fishing with a mate
oth whacking out, say, three rods apiece all around the boat,
to find all the floats and consequently the baits, huddled
her in just one small area of the lake. It's not exactly making
se of the potential area around the boat, which is the whole
of going afloat in the first place. And, of course, it's all due to
wind dragging your lines and floats along. So plan only to place
t-fished baits directly down wind of the boat. All the rest can
ply be free lined (which are unaffected by wind drift) with a
ple of swan shots on the trace so the pike has something to pull
inst and thus move off directly away from the boat and register
ositive bite. Also, to determine there are no arguments as to who
ould be fishing where, draw an invisible line either down the boat
ngthways, or across the middle (depending upon which way on to
e wind you have put the mud weights), and stick to your own half.

## 339 Hinged, galvanised steel anchors

Galvanised steel anchors of the hinged type are essential for securing firm anchorage in deep water when pike fishing the Scottish Lochs or in trout reservoirs. A 20 to 30 foot chain is attached at the lower, hinged end of the anchor shaft, before being run along the shaft and secured to the other end with a length of weak cord (that will break easily under pressure). It is then joined with enough rope to accommodate at least twice the depth of water beneath the boat. To retrieve the anchor, motor upwind and pull heavily to break the cord, after which the anchor is easily lifted from the roughest ground.

## 340 Casting across wind

A deadly method for catching both pike and zander in really windy weather from large sheets of still water is to cast directly across the wind (assuming you have anchored up with the bows into the wind) and allow a bow to form between your float fished live or dead bait and rod tip. Then, by paying out line gently, the float will work the bait directly down wind. Start with a cast close to the boat, and if nothing materialises along that particular drift (you can work the bait as far as the float remains visible), slowly retrieve and make the next cast a few yards further out and try another drift. It's a great way of systematically searching large sheets of especially, feature-less water.

## 341 Thick rubbing leaders

Whether casting lures or wobbling dead baits for pike from an anchored boat close to rocks incorporate a 20 foot thick mono rubbing leader between your wire trace and mainline.

# On the Drift and Trolling

## Invest in a drogue 342

Anyone who loves to boat fish on the drift using surface tow or the wind, will at some point find themselves at a distinct disadvantage without a drogue, whether fly fishing for trout or casting dead baits or artificial lures for pike. This relatively inexpensive item of tackle is usually constructed from rot-proof nylon or canvas and is attached around amidships to the windward side of the boat by rope or strong cord, often with a short length of galvanised steel chain at the drogue.

## Controlled fishing 343

Once your drogue is sunk below the surface and acting just like an underwater parachute, the boat's passage is considerably slowed down, so that fishing is done in a less hurried, more controlled manner. Thus the water is covered much more effectively.

## Run parallel to features 344

Here's a tip for would-be drogue users. When the drogue is tied on slightly off centre, more towards the stern or bows, the boat will crab across the wind. This enables it to run parallel with a particular feature such as a reed bed, island or the shoreline, rather than straight onto it. It's great fun, and makes for vastly more interesting and calculated fishing. Try it and see.

## Back-drifting abroad 3

Back-drifting - presenting small, live fish or fish strip bumping mer along the bottom 20-40 yards behind the boat - is a popular techni in tropical Africa on clear-flowing and clean, gravel-bottomed rivers like the Nile and the Zambezi, for both tiger fish and several species catfish. Along particularly deep reaches, a large swan shot or two is added to the wire trace immediately below the swivel to ensure the b is presented just above or actually bumping the river bed. And genera because the bottom is largely made up of clean shingle or sand, baits rarely become snagged.

## Back-drifting in the UK 34

Back-drifting also scores with pike and zander along many of our clear-flowing British rivers, when presenting dead baits, particularly where the bottom consists mainly of gravel or silt. Use a non-stretch, braided reel line in conjunction with a multiplying reel, so that free line can instantly be given to a taking fish by a simple click with the heel of your thumb. You need, however, to row or motor quickly upriver to release your terminal gear whenever the bait becomes snagged. Enormous lengths of river can be explored in this manner.

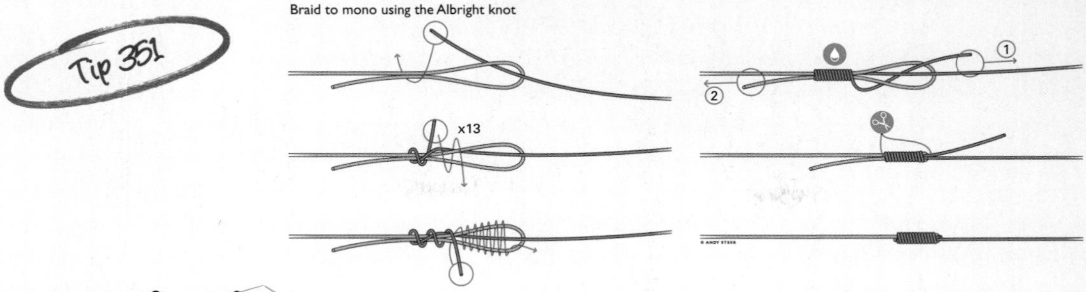


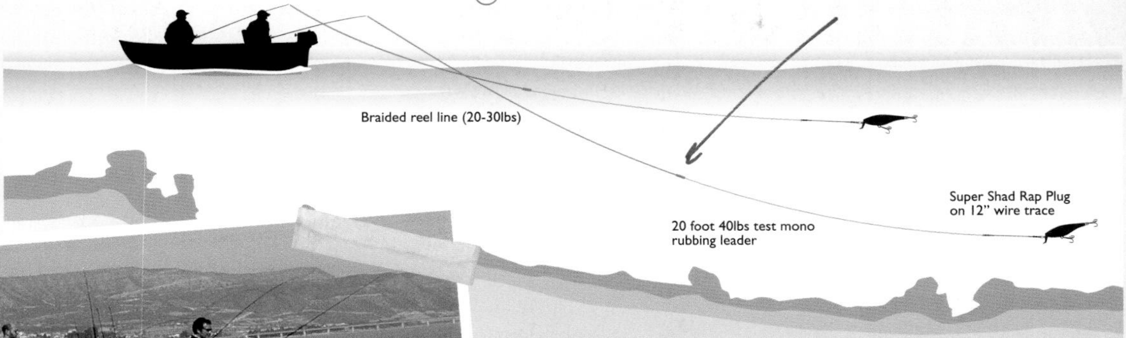

## he right angles

347

ack-drifting along with the current, presenting float-fished ve baits 10-30 yards behind the boat is another effective way f accounting for pike. To keep the boat side-on to the current hroughout the drift, one angler sits on the centre seat and jently works the oars. Remember to keep a mud weight at the ready so it can be instantly lowered within seconds of a pike grabbing one of the baits, so a more thorough search of the area can subsequently be made. Pike do tend to group-up in rivers in choice lies, so make the most of these situations.

## Freshwater trolling

348

Freshwater trolling, save for reservoir and loch fishing, is not regularly practiced in the UK. It is not permitted for instance on the Norfolk Broads, or throughout our networks of rivers and canals. But wherever you are allowed to pull an artificial lure behind a motor-powered boat, remember that due to its much thinner diameter, a braided line will allow any given artificial lure to dive significantly deeper than it would being attached to monofilament of identical breaking strain.

## Be alert to regular taps

349

When trolling artificial lures, spoons, diving plugs, etc and regular taps and short bangs on the rod tip fail to develop into solid hits, take the rod from its rest and immediately following the next tap, click the reel out of gear (multipliers are the only reels to use for trolling). Give a two or three yards of line (so the lure in effect momentarily stands still) before winding back into gear and cranking the lure forward fast. Whether you're after pike or big trout, or abroad targeting Nile perch or the legendary tiger fish, this ruse often results in a slamming take. So be ready.

## Forget rod holders

350

Holding the rod when trolling often produces bonus fish which would otherwise not be caught. Rod holders can make you lazy. Get used to continually fishing shorter or longer lines, especially around headlands for instance, where fish tend to congregate at the corners and dropping the lure back, or shortening the line accordingly whilst watching the fish finder read out. Similarly, if you are holding the rod when trolling a lure close to or amongst snags, you'll have a much better chance of subsequently landing the fish.

## The Albright knot

351

When trolling in freshwater over a rocky bottom using a braided reel line, incorporate a 20 foot thick mono rubbing leader between your wire trace and mainline. Tie braid to thick mono using the Albright knot - a super-neat and strong knot which passes easily through level wind of multiplier reel. See diagram above.

Freshwater Boat Fishing

# On the Drift and Trolling

## Study shorelines 352

Wherever you fish in the world, one way of ascertaining whether water levels are up or down, even in a flooded desert environment such as Egypt's Lake Nasser shown here, is to study the shoreline. Look at the different lines of grasses and bushes that have sprung up from seeds washed up on the shore when the lake was at previous heights.

## Avoid tangles 353

Try not to troll a mixture of mono and braided reel lines. If they come together, long, twisted tangles will result.

## Watch floating plugs 354

When letting out floating/diving plugs, keep them in your sight whilst line pulls freely, without any thumbing from the spool, until each is the desired distance behind the boat. Then click the reel into gear and allow each lure to dive. You then know their exact distance from the boat. If you thumb whilst they are going out, they will dive and you'll lose sight of them, not knowing how far behind the boat each is running.

## Lenses for dark conditions 35

Don't forget the Polaroid glasses when out afloat, especially in dull and extremely overcast conditions. Yes, especially when light values are low, for which HLT yellow lenses are indispensable. In clear water conditions you will actually be able to see pike following a lure or wobbled dead bait right up to the boat, and observe areas of dense weed.

## Lenses for bright conditions 356

For bright and sunny conditions when the surface is calm, wear grey or amber lens Polaroids for reducing reflective glare, and a peaked cap.

## Mud weights 3

Keep a mud weight at the ready even when trolling or drifting, and slip it ov the side immediately you hook up and start playing the fish. You can then co the area thoroughly by casting around, trying a variety of lures before restart the drift or the motor for trolling.

## Electric motors 35

Electric motors that work from a heavy-duty battery and via their G clamp can virtually be clipped on anywhere around the boat are indispensable. They correct the line of drift every so often and they are also great for trolling over popular areas where the fish become used to, and consequently spooked by, the sound and vibrations of petrol outboard motors.

## atch the depths 359

hilst it's nice to mark fish congregated ound sunken features when trolling using sonar/fish finder, pay most attention to the tual depths prior to and immediately after ch feature shown on the display screen, and ork your lures at according depths. There is evitably a hot zone where one of the lures s grabbed as you pass through. Finding it is more important than relying on fish symbols hown on the display screen.

## Monitor vibrations 360

Whenever one of the rod tops stops vibrating to the particular lure it is trolling, wind in immediately to inspect. The tiniest strand of weed can impair the lure's action, resulting in no hits.

## Impromptu drogues 361

You may be out for a day pike fishing in gentle winds when you decide to try drift fishing but you do not own a drogue. Here, dangle your keep net (with a rock inside) behind the boat on the windward side, tied on firmly around the rowlocks. It will considerably slow down the boat.

3

# The FINAL YARD

• Rods and Reels • Lines • Sundries • Hooks and Rigs

"Be a yardstick of quality. Some people aren't used to an environment where excellence is expected."

# Rods and Reels

## Go American for bait casting 362

For some really exciting pike, zander, perch and chub fishing, invest in a little American-style, pistol grip, bait-casting outfit. Rods are tip-actioned and one piece, just 6-7 feet long, and work beautifully using a single-handed casting action, with a baby multiplying reel. Such an outfit allows you to place plugs and spoons etc, close alongside weed rafts or beneath overhanging trees, or along reed-lines with extreme accuracy. This technique relies on mobility, stealth and observation and is particularly suited to small still waters and river fishing during the summer and autumn months. So wear Polaroid glasses, drab clothes and take along only the bare essentials stored in your waistcoat. Then you'll enjoy walking for miles.

## Avoid breakages 363

Snapping the top two or three inches of a finely tapered quiver tip rod, is in all probability the most common breakage amongst every type of freshwater rod. This is because the reel line usually becomes wrapped around the second (tiny) ring prior to casting whilst baiting up, as the line goes slack. To alleviate this, get used to gently pulling on the line between reel and butt ring immediately before each and every cast. If the line is wrapped you will feel it. Simply lower your end rig onto the ground and shake the rod tip while gently pulling the line between reel and butt ring, until it comes free. Alternatively, ensure the line is tight and your quiver tip slightly bent whilst baiting or filling the feeder, so the line cannot coil around the end of the tip.

## Optimum lures 364

To obtain optimum performance in terms of lure action and subsequent hooking-up when working jigs and jerkbaits you need a specialised rod and reel outfit. The ideal rod should be stiffish, no longer than 6-7 feet with an acute tip action. Such rods are designed to be used with a 6000-6500 sized multiplier and therefore held upside down. This means that if you are right handed, you need a left-hand wind reel, so that your strong arm works the rod. To ensure every flick of the rod tip is transferred to the artificial lure, a non-stretch, low-diameter braided reel line of between 30-50lbs test is imperative. This may seem excessive, but some jerk baits are both heavy and large and the continual casting demands a lot of your reel line. And as braid is so much thinner than mono (less than half the diameter), it's better to err on the safe side. Besides, with stronger reel line, it is easier to pull an expensive lure free from most snags without the fear of breaking off.

## 365 Repairing the rods

Should you snap a few inches off the top of a built-in quiver tip rod, you'll need to replace the solid glass or carbon tip. Start by carefully removing the whipping around the junction with a razor blade or craft knife. This will reveal if the tip is sleeved through the rod's top joint and pulled out the end, or is merely pushed in from the top. Some manufacturers actually glue the tip in, in which case you'll need to cut back the end of the joint to remove the two to three inches of glued-in quiver tip, and then gently chamfer the end with a file to facilitate an even whipping, before fitting a new quiver tip. Keep all the rings of the old tip so they can be whipped onto the replacement. You will, however, need to buy a new tip ring, which simply pushes and glues on. Most manufacturers produce replacement tips, but for those that do not, buy a 30-36 inch solid glass Donkey top and sleeve through the top joint until it protrudes from the end. Pull gently through and twist until it locks into place, then mark the spot with a pencil. Judge how much needs to be cut off from the thick end (use a fine tooth hacksaw blade for cutting) by coming back around two inches from your pencil mark and gently saw through. Pull through and twist again to lock into position, before making a whipping over the junction, and then whip on the rings. If the tip is too fine, gently cut back to your requirements before obtaining a new tiny, push on tip ring and fixing with a touch of superglue. Now, should you ever break the new tip; it can be removed easily and a replacement fitted without having to cut the tip back again and alter the action of the rod. To finish, paint around 18 inches of the tip in matt white, with a two-inch band of bright red at the extreme end, for maximum visibility of tiny bite registrations in dull conditions.

## 366 Protect spinning and fly rods

When fishing abroad and several flights in light aircraft are required to reach secluded locations, three and four piece spinning and fly rods packed in a protective tube are worth their weight in gold.

## 367 Understanding rod test curves

Many rods are marked in their respective test-curves, which provides you, the customer, with an idea as to their power and what strength lines should be used. The late Dick Walker devised this useful guideline, which works simply by multiplying the rod's test curve by the number 5. So a rod with a 2lbs test curve for instance, works perfectly in harmony with a 10lbs test monofilament line. Braided reel lines incidentally, do not come into any of these equations. To find the lowest breaking strain monofilament line that the rod will comfortably handle, multiply by 4 (8lbs test), and for its upper limit multiply by 6, which is 12lbs test. This does not naturally mean that lighter or heavier lines cannot be used in particular circumstances. It merely provides a useful guideline.

## 368 Multiplier reels

Small multiplier reels are an absolute joy to use due to their light weight, neat, smallness of size (compared to many fixed spool monstrosities) silky-smooth clutch and the fact that the line is wound directly onto the spool without passing around a bale arm roller (like a fixed spool reel). And not only for lure fishing, the purpose for which they were initially devised. All manner of freshwater situations are arguably improved by opting to use a baby multiplier instead of the traditional fixed spool reel. I use multipliers for much of my pike fishing (the ratchet becomes an instant bite alarm when the reel is in free spool, as it does when bolt-rig ledgering for carp) and for both float and general ledgering tactics for carp and barbel, even tench.

## 369 Carp on a multiplier

To catch carp on the float at close range using a multiplier, line is simply pulled (using two fingers) from either side of the butt ring as I would do with a centre-pin reel, and an underarm or sideways cast is made to where bubbles or tail patterns are erupting on the surface. When on, a big carp can be played noticeably closer to the breaking strain of the line, using a heavy drag setting, than with a fixed spool reel, because the line comes directly off and is wound straight back onto the spool (no line twist either incidentally) without travelling at right angles around a bale arm. Try it and see for yourself.

## 370 The best reel tip

For most close-range float fishing techniques in both running and still waters, get yourself a centre-pin reel. For long trotting it is simply unrivalled and provides direct and perfect control over any float because you can easily slow down the float (and your bait) by applying gentle thumb pressure to the revolving drum. Quality centre pins are even fitted with a micro-adjustable disc drag (which puts pressure upon the spindle) for mechanically slowing the reel down in really fast currents, and have a built-in line guard to stop coils of line slipping behind the cage when fishing in slow rivers during windy conditions. And for playing big fish, since the line leaves the reel in a straight line (as opposed to going at right angles around a bale arm as with all fixed spool and closed face reels), line twist is never a problem.

Freshwater Tackle

# Rods and Reels

## Forget line clips 371

Line clips, nowadays fitted into the side of the spool on the majority of fixed spool reels, are not always reliable. A big fish can easily steam off and snap the line when it is clipped up. The answer? Well it may be old hat, but try a simple tight-fitting elastic band slightly smaller in diameter than the spool and placed around it. This will not only prevent you casting beyond the baited area from which bites are coming (the reason for clipping up in the first place), it will permit any whopper to keep on going and rip line off without the fear of breakage.

## The Wallis cast 372

For the Wallis cast, originally devised for casting directly from the reel and trotting a heavily shotted float down fast rivers, a line guard is not required because the constant pull from strong currents stops line from flapping behind the cage. The impetus required however for starting the Wallis cast demands a reel line of at least 5lbs test. Use a firm sideways swing of the rod and heavily shotted float rig to send it distances of 20 yards or further across big rivers like the Hampshire Avon, for which the cast was developed. A 2lbs reel line would instantly snap. So while heavy lines of say up to 12-15lbs test can be used on both types of reel for catching carp or pike, if you wish the facility of stepping down every so often to just a 2lbs reel line for sensitive float fishing in slow moving rivers as well as fishing heavier, then choose a centre pin with a built-in line guard. If, however, you will not be stepping below lines of 5lbs test, and mainly fishing fast flowing rivers, a centre pin without a line guard is perfect for you.

## Compact fixed spool reels 373

Now that relatively compact fixed spool reels (size 3000 downwards) are available with a bait-runner or free-spool facility, and competitively priced too, it makes sense to use them. The free-spool switch, usually located at the rear of the reel, instantly disengages the spool's drag, so that line can be stripped from the rotating spool at a tension of your setting (via a calibrated knob) by a pike or a carp having belted off with the bait (hence the original term bait runner) without the rod being dragged in. And as you might be using this sensitive facility for any number of techniques such as ledgering for perch, pike or zander, free lining for catfish or eels, bolt rig ledgering for carp, tench, chub, bream or barbel, or simply float fishing for carp, and you don't fancy the rod disappearing into the lake when you stand up to make a call of nature, any slight extra purchase cost seems irrelevant.

## Your style determines your reel and rod 374

Here's a most important tip if you are considering purchasing, or indeed if you already own, a free-running centre-pin reel. How you intend casting, either Nottingham or Wallis style, reflects the type of reel and rod that you require. With Nottingham casting, for instance, where fingers of line (like a spider's web) are pulled from between reel and butt ring and from between up to each of the first three rings above, (depending upon how far you wish to cast), you need a reel that has a built-line guard. This stops line flapping behind the cage in windy conditions when trotting a float along slow-moving rivers. Choose a float rod therefore, already fitted with three rings set close together on the butt section to accommodate centre pin fishing. Or whip a couple more on the rod you own.

AnglingTimes
INSIDE THIS WEEK
ALL-NEW FISH CALCULATOR
World's greatest roach fishery
FREE

# Rods and Reels

## Feathering — 375

When casting with a fixed spool reel and whether ledger or float fishing, get used to the art of feathering the line against the side of the spool using your forefinger, in order to brake the cast and bring the float or feeder down exactly where you want it. Feathering also makes the bait precede the float so it comes to land ahead of the float in exactly the desired spot. Practice makes perfect here.

## Front drags — 376

It's a fact that fixed spool reels with front drags (with tension nut on the spool itself) are actually smoother than those with rear drags, though they might not look so space age.

## All-through action rods — 377

Whether you choose a rod with a light (1¼lbs) test curve, or a heavy (2½lbs) model, those with an all-through action will not only allow you to enjoy the fight more, but also put your fish on the bank surprisingly quickly. This is without the risk of the hook pulling or the line snapping when the fish is under the rod tip on a short line and decides to make a last ditch dive, which is why fly rods are so incredibly effective. They just keep bending and bending to the lunges of the largest fish. So be careful when selecting a new rod. Decide whether you want it for close to medium range fishing, or for distance work.

## Avon-style rods — 378

The most versatile tool covering most aspects of fresh water fishing is the Avon-style rod, which has a test curve of around 1¼lbs. It will handle monofilament lines ranging from 5 up to 8lbs test and as such will easily subdue, due to its all-through action, all but the most heavyweight of carp, pike and catfish.

## Hold firmly — 379

Get used to holding your rod and (fixed spool) reel firmly and comfortably so it becomes part of your forearm. Start by laying your strong arm along the rod butt and placing your hand around the reel stem with two fingers gripping on either side. Your forefinger will now be perfectly situated for picking up the line when you open the bale arm to cast, for applying pressure to the side of the spool when playing a big fish, and for feathering the line down when casting.

## No need for rod rests — 380

To hold your rod steady for fishing the lift and waggler methods whilst sitting down, without use of a rod rest, the bottom of your reel should be touching your knee, whilst your forearm presses the rod's handle along your thigh. If held correctly, you can actually ease up on your grip around the reel fitting, as it is your forearm which keeps everything steady. Your hand will certainly tighten up quickly enough when the float moves.

## Changing the slipping clutch — 381

When playing big fish using a fixed spool reel, you will probably need to alter the setting of the slipping clutch several times during the fight. Really ease up (slacken off) when that monster is on a short line under the rod tip and your left hand is busy wielding the landing net, because if the fish makes one last dive on a firm clutch setting either the line will break or you will rip the hook out. A non-stretch, braided reel line only accentuates this potential problem.

# Cats 'N" Carp on the Famous River Ebro - Come Fishing with the Real Experts!

*Bavarian Guiding Service*

In our 21st year now, we are the longest established guiding service onthe Rio Ebro System. Our six full-time resident angling guides have over 80 years of experience fishing for catfish, carp, and zander. No wonder that an amazing number of our guests return year after year to sample what is

## THE BEST CATFISHING IN THE WORLD!

With a choice of accommodation and guiding options, you simply tell us what you would like and we will do out best to come up with a package to suit. Prices start at 350 euros per angler (based on a party of 3) for a week's stay in our Scandinavian timber cabins on the banks of the Rio Segre. This includes all licenses and exclusive use of a motor-boat. Our large fleet of top-quality craft are conveniently moored at the camp's private boatstages and offer you the freedom to fish wherever you like.Parties of anglers, or family groups, are easily accommodated for in our luxury villas, available on both the Mar de Aragon (The Upper Lake) and in Mequinenza. All are situated close to idyllic fishing spots and **WORLD-CLASS FISHING**. We have 4 recently modernised riverside apartments which are literally a few feet from the Rio Ebro. All packages include a fishing boat for the duration of your visit. Carp anglers too have discovered the incredible sport on offer at the International Fishing Camp. Huge numbers of big carp are caught throughout the season, but **WINTER IS THE PRIME TIME** for top carp sport – many fish are well over forty pounds and they keep getting bigger. Multiple catches of hard fighting river carp in excess of thirty pounds are commonplace! Special price Winter carp deals are available from mid-November–just give us a call or e-mail and we will give you

**THE BEST POSSIBLE PRICE.**

For all enquiries contact Mike on 0207 060 2143 (Office). Alternatively you can e-mail at **mike@spanish-catfish-ebro.com**. Why not visit our website at **www.spanish-catfish-ebro.com.**

**10% Discount for CCG Members**

tackle.com bgs

20 years Catching Fish since 1988

# nternational Fishing Camp

# Sundries

## 382 Essential bait droppers

If I were to choose the most beneficial of the countless sundries that in one form or another have a real and valuable use in my fishing, it would be the simple bait dropper. They are constructed from a variety of materials including high-density plastic, brass and stainless steel. There are tiny models no larger than a matchbox for depositing half a handful of maggots or casters down to the river bed when I'm roach and grayling fishing, as well monster units that can drop half a pint of hempseed onto the gravel bottom of a fast-flowing river when barbel are the target species.

## 383 PVA

A comparatively modern material that I also find invaluable is PVA. I use both bags and the mesh tubing for ensuring that my hook bait lies on the bottom surrounded by free offerings. And in achieving this, PVA has no equal.

## 384 Match-fishing scissors

For ease of chopping up worms for adding to ground bait, obtain a pair of match-fishing style scissors with multiple blades. There is nothing easier.

## 385 Peacock quills

Plain peacock quills with or without their herl (us for fly tying) are by far the most useful float material around. Simply cut to the desired length with a pair of scissors. Add a half-inch band of colour, fluorescent orange or red to the top of a 3-6 inch section and secure to your line at the base with a band of silicone rubber. And to a fish looking upwards through clear water, what could look more natural floating in the surface film than a bird quill?

## 386 Quills for lift fishing

Due to its inherent buoyancy (one inch of slim quill will support a BB shot) a peacock quill is by far the best float for lift fishing, because whilst the float is rising it is actually supporting the single swan shot fixed on the line just a few inches above the hook. So don't wait for the float to lie flat before striking, because by then the fish will be supporting the shot.

## 387 Preparing quills

Half a dozen peacock quills will set you back less than four commercially-made floats, yet when cut up into 4-6 inch sections, they will provide dozens of floats. Simply colour the top half inch of one end in either red or orange fluorescent paint, and fix to the line with a section or two of silicon float rubber.

## Cheap quills 388

Because peacock quills are so cheap, you won't mind losing floats that pop out of the band when carp or tench go charging through lilies or dense weed beds. It's far better than the line snapping with a crack when the shots either side of a commercially-made waggler restrict a fish's passage through aquatic plants.

## Washing up liquid 389

Keep a small bottle of neat washing up liquid in your kit for occasions (such as waggler fishing) when your line won't sink. Splodge a forefinger full around the line on the reel spool and wipe your hand thoroughly before baiting up.

## pecial scissors 390

small pair of sharp scissors ept close to hand not only aves on tooth enamel, but trims monofilament line neatly. To trim braided lines, you need a pair of specialised braid scissors.

## ightweight waistcoats 391

Visually locating your fish by stalking is made all the easier by carrying the absolute minimum of tackle. So rather than a box or holdall full of everything you might need, wear a lightweight waistcoat housing exactly what you do need. Think about it.

## ear trainers when stalking 392

dry conditions when stalking around a e or along a river bank for extra spooky ecies, leave the wellies or waders back in e car. A pair of lightweight old trainers eate far less vibrations.

Freshwater Tackle

# Sundries

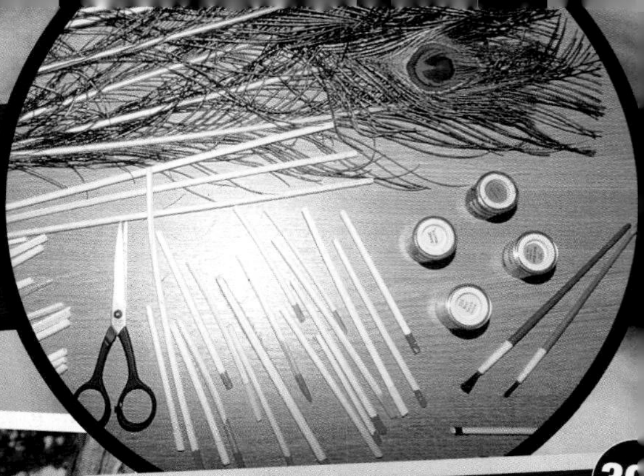

## Buy a compact digital camera 39

For capturing that trophy photo, particularly when you ha miles to walk and your camera bag weighs a ton, a small, modern digital camera with a rating of around 4-5 millio pixels, that fits snugly into your top pocket, is worth its w in gold. See also, Saltwater Tackle Sundries, Tips 6, 7 and

## Camera thread adaptors 39

Most digital compacts have a screw thread in the base to accept a tripod. But this is only more clutter to carry arou For just a few quid (from your specialist tackle shop) you c purchase a camera thread adaptor which at one end screv into the base of the camera, and at the other, into a bank stick. So you can easily photograph yourself with the fish lifetime, should there be no one else around.

## Use the self timer 39

If purchasing a new compact digital camera, ensure it has self-timer mode in the menu. Some give you the choice of just one or three pics (with a 10-second delay in between) just one press of the shutter release button. This feature is desirable for self-photography because whilst the first sho usually gets wasted due to picking a big fish up and taking to hold it square onto the camera lens, numbers two and th capture the moment perfectly. Job done.

## Get comfortable 39

Self photography becomes easier if you sit on your box or chair when displaying your fish to the camera. Set the camera up on the bank stick around waist height, several feet away, making sure the stick is perfect upright, so that the bottom of the frame cuts off your legs below the kn Try a dry run with a pic or two, positioning your hands to either the rig or left (simulating holding the fish), which gives a better depth of field ar ensures the main subject will be in sharp focus. And slowly lift your arm above your knees so you know what level they need to be at and take a If all's well, do it for real.

397

## -paring rods

-king up a rod or two the evening before has caught me an awful -f big fish over the years (covering the location and species to targeted in the morning). I then break them down again with -elastic band securing the line and joints at each end, for instant -ection and use apart from adding the bait. In fact, only when -ravelling abroad do I put them in rod bags and into a protective tube.

398

## A varied tackle selection

My tackle room is full of varying pre-made outfits, covering fly fishing, lure fishing, pike dead baiting, carp, long trotting etc. So all I have to do is grab the right set-ups and go.

399

## Ready rigs are quick and quiet

Erecting your ready-rigged rod on the bank within seconds not only saves time, but also all that extra noise emanating from carrying a rod holdall, taking rods from their bags, moving about the bank fitting them together etc, all of which simply tells the fish you have arrived. I say you'll catch more, certainly larger, spookier fish and quicker, by having your rods pre-made. Try it and see.

400

## Pre-mades at night

You can even erect a pre-made rod in the dark by holding it up to the sky when fixing joints together to alleviate the line from going around the spigots, and be making the first cast of the day without your quarry being even slightly aware of your presence.

401

## The right waistcoat

To follow on from my way of being ready at the drop of a hat, I also have a selection of different waistcoats, some light, some with thermal linings, each loaded with a different selection of sundry items particular to the species I might be after. I do not own a comprehensive seat-type tackle box or bag as such.

# Lines

## Sink the line 402

When waggler float fishing in still water, it is imperative to sink the line between float and rod tip in order to counteract any draw or sub-surface tow. This is so you can pull the line through the surface tension, (simply by striking sideways) as opposed to lifting it up against it. Cast a little further than you are baiting the target area therefore, and feather the line down (by using your forefinger against the spool) before dropping the rod tip a few inches beneath the surface and cranking the reel handle like mad for a few turns. This not only sinks but also straightens the line out. New lines benefit from sloshing a little washing up liquid (keep a small bottle handy) around the spool prior to fishing, or you can deliberately purchase lines which sink.

## Monitor your line condition 40

It is false economy to fish with line that has been on your reel for so long it has deteriorated either through sunlight (ultra violet rays affect monofilament severely) or such constant use, as most of the line's inherent elasticity has gone. Every time you get caught up on a snag a pull for a break, the last few yards of a monofilament line may have be taken beyond its point of elasticity, rendering it useless. So don't simpl tie another hook on the end. Keep cutting the end back until the line shows no sign of abrasion and when stretched, immediately returns. I any doubt, change the line completely for fresh.

## Braided lines 40

Whilst incredibly strong in breaking strain for their low diameter, braided lines need to be thoroughly scrutinised regularly (with a magnifying glass if necessary) so that any section which shows the slightest sign of deterioration such as furring or roughness, where it has passed over rocks or tree branches etc, can be instantly discarded. Being much thinner than monofilament (less than half the diameter for any given breaking strain) it takes but a slight nick in a braided line for a breakage to inexplicably occur.

## Dealing with sudden breakages 405

Whenever inexplicable and sudden breakages occur whilst float fishing with monofilament, first check your main line by running it between your thumb and forefinger to feel for any roughness that indicates deterioration, caused by rubbing against tough plant stems or rocks, etc. And just in case the problem is with your rod, check all the rings carefully, especially the tip ring for any cracks or abrasive areas.

## Check elasticity 406

Another way of testing monofilament for deterioration is to hold the line tightly in your hands about two feet apart and firmly pull to test for its degree of elasticity. If it snaps before you think it should, then replace immediately. Pinching large locking shots onto fine monofilament is often the cause of breakage. Either get used to pinching them on lightly, or protect the line beneath large shots by sleeving onto the line 5-8mm lengths of fine diameter silicon tubing (used for attaching pole floats) which act as padding when you pinch your shots around them.

Tip 408

Forming a 'stringer' loop for retaining big fish – Catfish, Nile Perch, Mahseer etc

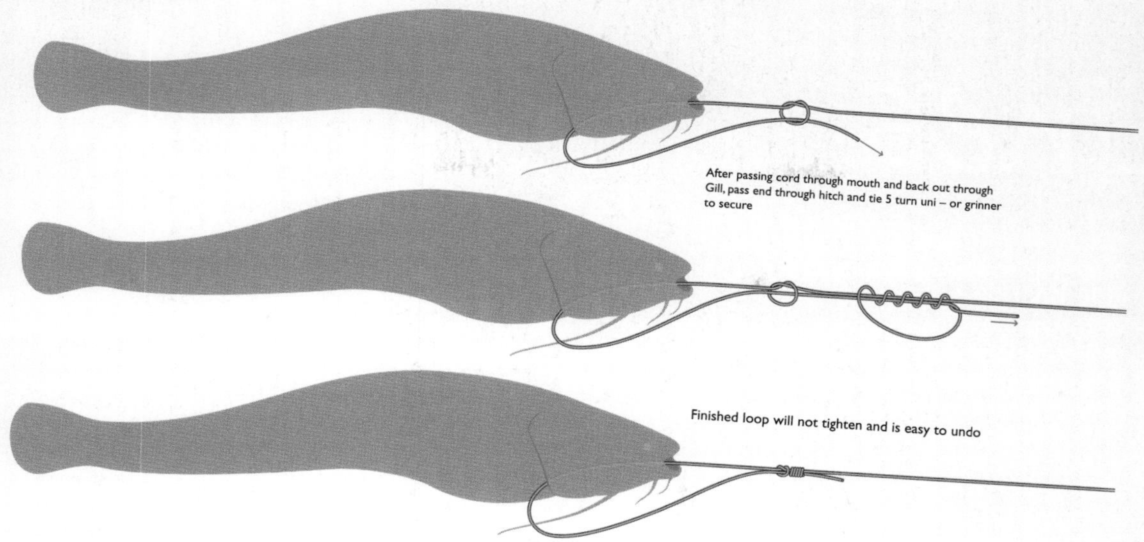


## Nylon cord 407

For making a stringer to retain large fish when abroad such as Nile perch, mahseer, arapaima, or Wels catfish, invest in some thick but supple strong, nylon cord. Parachute lines sold at Army surplus shops will do at a pinch, although catfish specialist shops also supply the ideal material. What is most important is to be able to form a large loop (which passes through the fish's mouth and out through its gill opening) that will not tighten while the fish is retained with the end of the rope tied to a bush, tree or stake.

## Stringer loop 408

To form the stringer loop, start by tying a single hitch 2-3 feet from the end of the cord. Now thread the cord through the fish's mouth and out through its gill opening. Be careful not to disturb the rakers. Now pass the tab end through the hitch you made and tie a five-turn grinner or uni knot around the cord. See diagram above. Tighten down against the hitch, and you have a large loop that cannot possible tighten any smaller. Practice a few times to make perfect.

## Line colour 409

The jury is still out on the subject of which colour line spooks fish least, because there is in fact no answer. Whatever the colour of your line, fish are all too aware that it exists. And thank goodness they do. If they didn't, can you imagine the amount of line bites we would all be continually suffering? Presenting a bait amongst shoal species would be hell, with indications on the float or bobbin happening all the time, as indeed they do when large species such as tench and carp are spawning. Truth is that, however painful it may seem, fish do see and are aware of our lines, which is how for most of the time they manage to avoid it.

## Friction weakens lines 410

Remember, even the most expensive monofilament line weakens severely and quickly through heat caused by friction. This is due to pulling shots or a float (held on by silicon bands) quickly up and down a dry line, or tying knots and pulling on them without adding a lubricant such as saliva.

## Buy line in bulk 411

It makes economical sense to buy your line in bulk so you don't have to worry whether a spool will be filled sufficiently by just a 100 yard spool. And because bulk line costs less, you will be more inclined to change regularly from old to new. But remember to store your bulk spools in the dry and preferably in the dark, because if left open to sunlight the monofilament could spoil through ultra violet rays.

# Lines

## Extreme heat and elasticity 412

When using heavier strains of monofilament abroad in extreme heat, where even rods not in use are in holders open to full sunlight, some brands of mono cam actually start to deteriorate within just a week. In such conditions, it's worth checking their suppleness and elasticity on a daily basis.

## Braided reel line specifics 41

While braided reel lines have improved certain techniques due
their inherent lack of elasticity and extremely low diameter, exa
these two factors must be kept in mind at all times. For instanc
when drift-float fishing for pike, runs can be effectively struck
the line regularly mended against the wind at distances up to a
100 yards. But 10 minutes later when that big pike has been pla
close into the margins and when held on a short line, decides to
make one last powerful dive beneath the rod tip, one of two thin
will happen: either the hooks will be ripped out, or the wire trace
braided line will snap.

## Thick mono rubbing leaders 414

Incorporate a 20 foot thick mono rubbing leader starting immediately above the hook trace for dealing with rocky and particularly snaggy bottoms whilst fishing for barbel in deep and fast-flowing rivers, particularly during flood time. This accomplishes two things. It will keep the amount of line fractures amongst the rocks to a minimum, whilst the five-turn double grinner or uni knot connecting leader to your mainline (providing you don't trim the ends too short) acts as a collecting depot for weed and other flood debris that would otherwise work its way down the line and around the terminal rig.

## Crimping 415

When ledgering for pike, zander or eels in tidal river systems - Norfolk's Great Ouse Relief Channel is a prime example - watch out for situations where quite suddenly your line falls back slack as though it has been bitten through above the terminal rig. Close inspection (you can often see and feel crimping along the line) will reveal that it has been nipped through by the sharp shells of Zebra mussels which grow in huge colonies.

## Sleeve on tubing 416

To alleviate the problems of Zebra mussels, sleeve fine diameter tubing over the last two to three feet of your reel line above the ledger rig, which might lay along the river bed and across Zebras.

## Change angles 417

Another way of avoiding the dreaded Zebras is to angle your rod tip up high (I know it inhibits bite registration) so most of your line is off bottom. Moreover, hit any run immediately. You cannot afford a fish to pull your reel line across the river bed and across Zebras'

Freshwater Tackle

# Lines

## Dealing with line twist 41

Following a powerful and lengthy battle with a big carp using monofilament line on a fixed spool reel, you are quite liable to suffer chronic line twist due to it being repeatedly pulled off the spool around a bale arm roller. Braided line incidentally doesn't suffer likewise because it has no elasticity. Sometimes this twisting of monofilament is so bad it's impossible to make another cast, leaving you two options. You either hack off all the twisted line and re-tie your rig (which is usually best), or you can run all the affected line out along the bank and let it flap about (taking most of the twist out) while you wind it back on the reel slowly. This at least eradicates some of the twist.

## Use centre-pin / mutiplier reels 419

By using either a centre-pin or multiplier reel, where the line is wound directly onto the spool and not via a bale arm roller, line twist simply doesn't occur.

## Anti-kink vane 420

Extreme line twist is also experienced by those who use spinners with blades that rotate at high speed (spoons and plugs merely wobble and chug), but there is a way of almost curing this. Simply incorporate a plastic (half moon shape) anti-kink vane or fold over lead into the spinning trace so all the twisting happens between it and the spinner.

## Opt for stretchy mono at close range 42

Avoid using low-stretch (lower diameter for their breaking st pre-stretched) monofilament lines for fishing at close range, and especially when coupled to a powerful, tip-actioned rod. It so easy to forget their greatly reduced elasticity and promptly snap up. Far better to use standard, stretchy mono on the ree and use the benefit of a lower diameter and low stretch mono your hook length, unless out and out distance fishing, where t benefits of low stretch mono are much appreciated.

Another
FISHING
YEAR
John Wilson's
FISHING DIARY
2
JANUARY
Catch it now at
AMAZON.CO.UK

Freshwater Tackle

# Hooks and Rigs

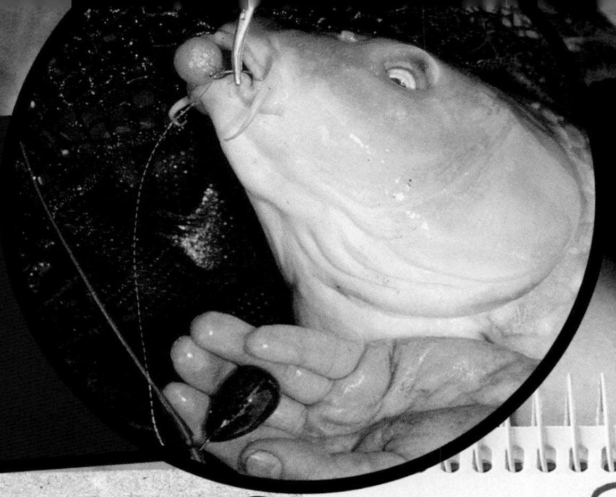

## Four-turn water knot 422

For joining a hook length (usually of a lighter breaking strain) to the main line when ledgering, many think that a loop-to-loop knot is best. But such a junction creates three separate weak spots, whereas a four-turn water knot creates only one. It's more of a weave really, making it stronger than a standard knot. See diagram.

## The Knotless Knot 423

Dubbed the knotless-knot and widely used by those presenting boilies or large pellets on a hair rig, it is a quick, all-in-one way of simultaneously attaching the hook and constructing a hair rig. This is because the line merely passes through and against the eye of the hook (it can be tied using either braid or monofilament). However, it should not be used with hooks where the eye is not fully closed, otherwise the line is prone to fracture in the gap under extreme pressure. Hooks of a seamless construction are available to alleviate this problem.

## The Knotless technique 424

To perform the knotless knot and attach the hook on say 20 inches of hook length material, start by forming a small loop at one end for the hair using a simple overhand knot. Now thread the other end down through the top of the hook's eye, and lay what will be the hair along the shank, ensuring that from the start of the bend, the hair, when pointed upwards, will be exactly the length desired to accommodate your boilie. See diagram Fig A. Now, wind the line in tight turns along the shank until you reach the bottom of the hair, and making one turn around it as in Fig B. Then wind it back again, passing the end up through the eye of the hook from below the eye, as in Fig C. And that's it, except for tying on your trace swivel, 8-12 inches away.

## Barrel Knot and hair rig 425

Another way of constructing an all-in-one hair rig and attachment of the hook when using 8-15lbs monofilament line, and you don't want knots at a swivel-junction to greatly reduce the breaking strain, is to use my barrel knot and hair rig shown in diagram. Start by threading the end of your reel line down through the top of the hook's eye and lay along the shank to form a 10 inch circle of line, with just half an inch of the tab end protruding beyond the bend, as in Fig A. Now, taking the right-hand side of the circle, between forefinger and thumb of your right hand, wind around shank and line 8 times going towards the eye (as in Fig B) and finish by pulling through tightly with the tab end. This forms a barrel knot along the shank which can be eased along tight up to the eye before pulling really tight, as shown in Fig C. Lastly, tie a simple overhand knot on the tab end to form the loop of your hair rig and trim off, as in Fig D. You now do not have a single knot acting as a weak link between rod tip and hook point. If you find the loop finicky to tie on hairs less than 1 1/2inches in length, sleeve a tiny crimp (used for wire traces) over the tab end to form a loop at the desired distance and firmly crimp at each end with round nosed pliers, before trimming off any surplice tab end.

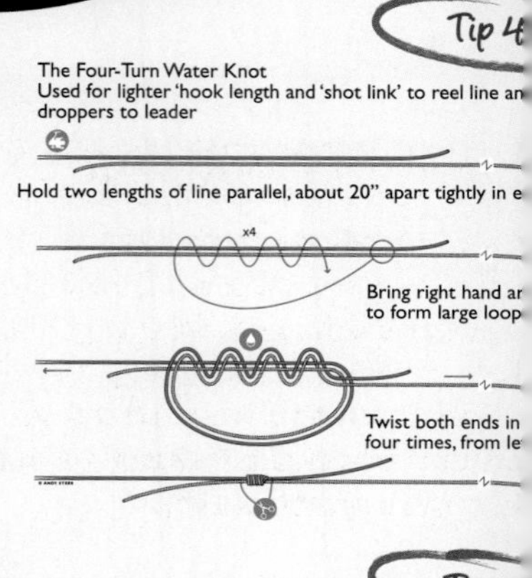


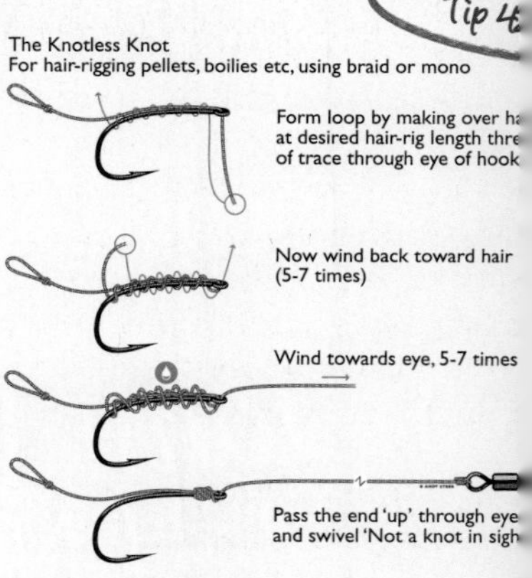


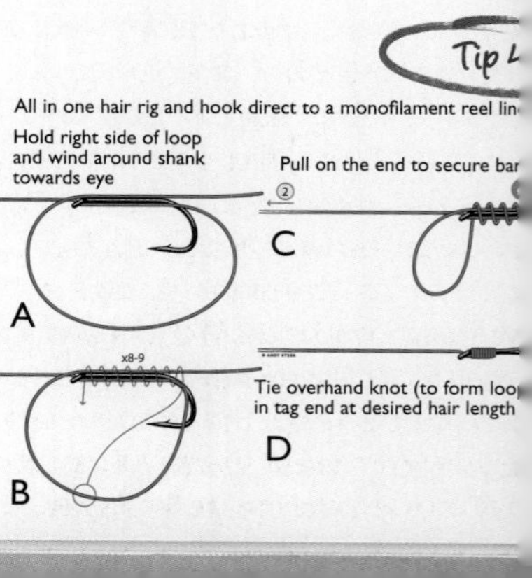

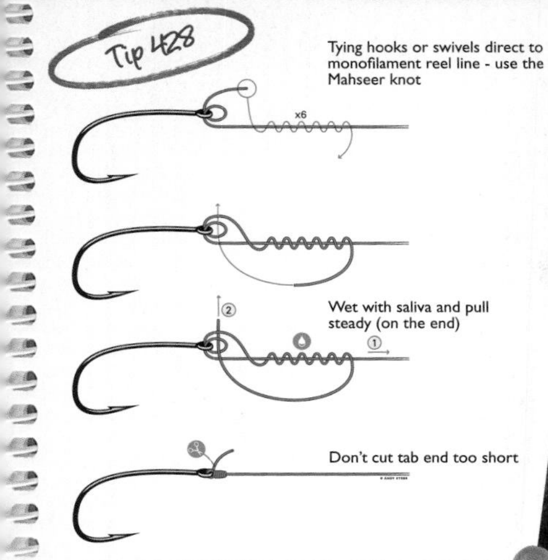

## ·da Maggot clip 426

·esenting a really large bunch of lively maggots on your hair rig ı after carp, tench, chub or barbel, the Korda Maggot Clip is a real This non-reflective device, slightly larger in diameter than a swan has a pointed end for sleeving maggots on without puncturing them ı, when full, is retained in a brooch-type mini clip. Your bunch of ots can then be added to the loop of your hook's hair rig or attached Korda Micro rig swivel in a jiffy.

## -clinch knot 427

ying an eyed hook or snap swivel to a braided reel line, my uni-clinch is both quick and easy to tie. As can be seen from the diagram, after ng the line through the eye twice and out again through the loop ı forms a simple clinch, use the tab end to tie a six-turn uni knot d the reel line (Fig A). Steadily pull on the tab end until the knot s a neat barrel (Fig B), and then pull slowly and firmly on the reel line so the barrel knot slides down along the reel line tight up against the . Then trim the end (Fig C).

## mahseer knot 428

ying all sizes of eyed hooks, from tiny size 18 up to giant 8/0 direct ur monofilament reel line, or adding swivels, there is no more reliable than the mahseer knot. Why? Because the knot itself actually ches under severe pressure, as opposed to constricting, which is the problem with many blood-type knots. To tie, pass the line twice gh the eye which forms a loop. Retain by putting your forefinger gh the loop and twist the tag end six times around the line, which s a second loop. Now pass the tag end through both loops next to ye, leaving a long tag end. Wet with saliva and pull steadily to bed down evenly. Also, pull steadily on long tag end to ensure it is firmly ed beneath both loops. Trim off tag end, but not too close. Now you lay the most powerful adversary as hard as you like knowing the will not inexplicably fracture. See diagram.

## Spade end hook 429

To tie a spade end hook direct to your reel line is simplicity itself. You certainly do not need a specialised tool. Start by laying the line along the shank of the hook (pointing towards the bend) and bring the tag end around in a 10 inch loop, so it protrudes just half an inch beyond the bend. See diagram Fig A. Now, holding the right side of the loop with your right hand (assuming you are right-handed), start winding back up along the shank towards the spade end (Fig B). After 8-9 turns, hold the knot tight beneath forefinger and thumb of your left hand, whilst pulling steadily on the tag end with your teeth or thumb and forefinger of your right hand. This forms a perfect barrel knot that can then be eased tight up against the spade end, and the tag end trimmed off, as in Fig C.

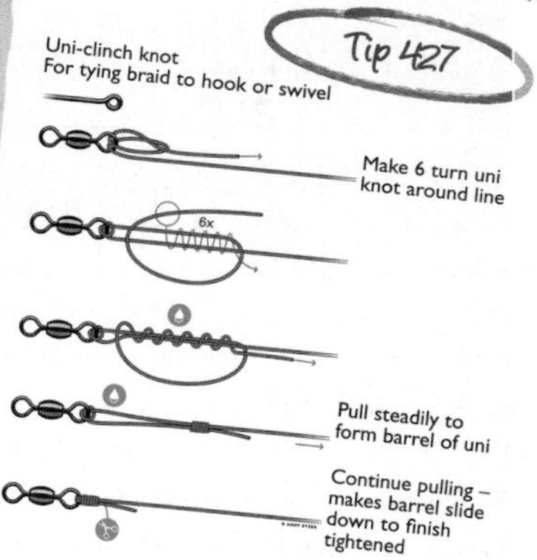


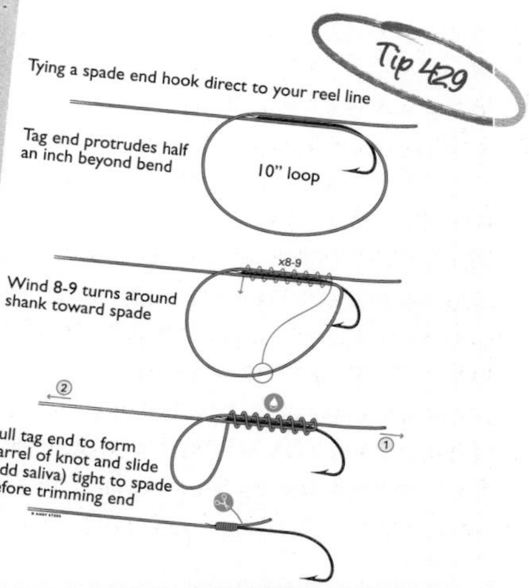

Freshwater Tackle

# Hooks and Rigs

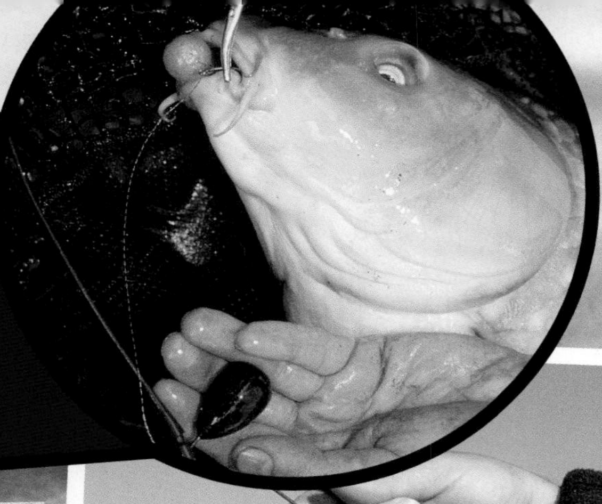

## Helicopter rig 430

A helicopter rig, favoured by many carp and tench anglers, is so called because the hook link is free to rotate around the main line above the lead or feeder tied directly to the end. To alleviate tangles, sleeve on 10 inches of fine diameter rubber tubing above the lead, and ensure the hook length is at least a couple of inches shorter.

## Fitting the helicopter 431

To fit the helicopter hook length, first sleeve a tight-fitting rubber bead onto the reel line and over the tubing, followed by the hook length swivel (which should be free to rotate) and then another bead, before tying reel line to lead or swivel. For a neat finish, push the end of the tubing over the lead or feeder swivel after tying to the reel line. To stop it sliding up the line, tie a five-turn sliding stop knot from 10-12lbs test power gum above it tight up against the tubing.

## Hair rigs 432

For the best chance of fish literally setting the hook themselves using the helicopter rig, present all baits from corn to boilies on a hair rig.

## Why in-line rigs? 433

In-line rigs, whether you use an in-line lead or an in-line frame feeder, benefit from the fact that a carp, tench, barbel or bream virtually hooks itself as it moves away with the bait. Should a line breakage occur, it won't become tethered to a snag because it will pull the line back through the lead or feeder.

## Setting up an in-line rig 434

Thread on 12-14 inches of fine diameter rubber tubing (which prevents the mainline rubbing against rocky bottoms and the hook trace tangling around the main line) and sleeve into the lead or feeder before tying on the hook trace swivel (usually a size 8) at the front end. This should then push firmly into the lead or frame feeder, making it a semi-fixed and completely safe rig. Finally, tie a five-turn stop knot using 10-12lbs test power gum tight up against the top end of the tubing to stop it sliding up the main line.

## Hook link length 43

The length of hook link for in-line rigs will depend upon to w extent the fish you are after are pressurised. Start with a leng of between just 4-6inches, especially if method-feeder fishing But on heavily fished waters, a 10 inch hook link will usually create less suspicion. Soft, braided hook lengths are preferre to stiffer monofilament. But the choice is yours.

## Hair rig when bolt-rig ledgering 436

All baits are best hair rigged when bolt-rig ledgering. If using a method frame feeder you can either leave your bait hanging below the feeder or mould the feed around the bait so it is part of the feeder's load. This can prove devastatingly effective, resulting in belting runs.

# Earn your 'stripes' with a big back-end perch

Whenever the end of a river fishing season approaches, it's well to remember that, as temperatures slowly rise, big perch can be added to the list of target species, along with those whopping great female dace, now pigeon-chested and liable to top the magical pound barrier. Then there's barbel, of course, which should really be enjoying a feeding spree after a particularly dormant winter.

That's the trouble with 'back-end' fishing. If the weather turns mild, just about everything in running water is on the cards, even a really big roach – yet there is little time left to capitalise on the situation. As far as big river perch are concerned, I like to keep my eyes on overnight temperatures because they are more likely to feed aggressively after several successive nights when the thermometer has kept well above freezing. So it's worth gathering a couple of hundred lobworms well in advance, so you can set off at the drop of a hat.

At the riverbank, look to explore all of those top 'habitat-hideout' swims where large bushes and trees overhang the water, creating darkness beneath. Also look for those long, thick lines of last summer's sedges, reed grass and bull rushes, all now brown and matted tightly over the surface of marginal swims; these are prime big-perch holding spots. A good yardstick to follow is that if a swim looks like a certain chub hotspot, it will, inevitably, contain perch – and sometimes both perch and chub of specimen proportions. Not on all rivers, of course. It doesn't seem to apply on my local River Wensum, for instance, which is not exactly known for its perch potential, although it does throw up a few nice fish between two and three pounds. However, many of my favourite swims along the upper reaches of the Great Ouse hold whacking great chub and perch. And, on the Ouse, you are looking at perch of three pounds and upwards, to even larger than the 4lbs beauty I'm holding here.

Strangely, the chub usually tend to be active when the perch are not – very cold weather being the leveller. Which I guess is why, when the perch are on the rampage and hoovering up a ledgered lobworm from the bottom – within seconds of it settling or my winding it several feet back up the swim and allowing it to flutter to the bottom again – I seem to attract few chub.

# Hooks and Rigs

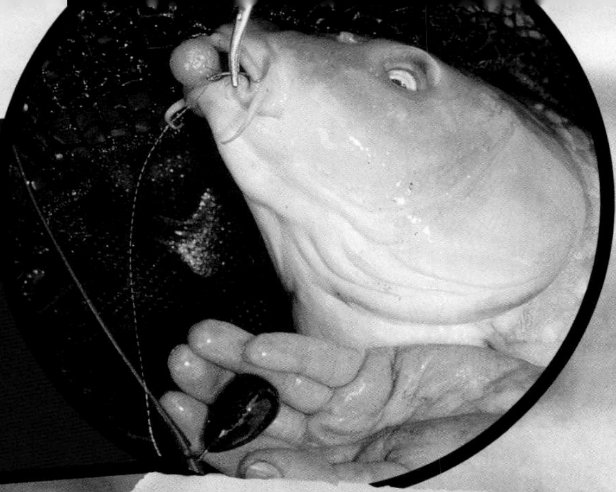

## Keep it simple to avoid suspicion 437

Never forget that the best rig of all, and one that creates the least amount of suspicion to a biting fish, is simply the baited hook tied direct to your reel line. Nothing more, nothing less. Add just a single swan shot and resistance is created. Add even more shots or a ledger weight and the problems are exaggerated.

## Teflon hooks 438

Nowadays, the choice in patterns of heavily forged hooks available to carp, tench and barbel anglers to complement bolt-rig ledgering techniques is simply marvellous, with neat, well-formed eyes, short shanks, micro barbs and super sharp, chemically etched points. And for the very best in hooks, it's worth going one step further by using patterns that come with a slick Teflon finish, in either gun metal or dull green. This non-reflective coating helps enormously in fooling the spookiest of fish.

## Micro barb hooks 439

I do not use barb-less hooks and actually prefer anglers visiting my own two-lake carp fishery to use relatively small hooks (sizes 10-8) with micro barbs. I think these, once embedded, move about less and cut less into the flesh of a carp's mouth especially during a long battle, or one in and out of dense weed, compared to larger, barb-less hooks.

## Pay attention 4

No-one likes to see grotesque examples of parrot-mouthed carp a tench. And the best way of ensuring this does not happen is to pa attention to what is happening. Do not fall asleep in a bivi, or walk round the other side of the lake when fishing close up to sunken tr dense lilies, or any other snag, because a hooked carp will naturally your heavy bolt rig and become stuck.

## Avoiding parrot-mouth fish 44

What actually creates so called parrot-mouth fish - where either one or both jaw hinges have been obliterated - is the see-saw cutting action of large hooks. Harsh, braided hook lengths, connected to over-heavy leads are literally ripped out of the mouth on heavy line, because the angler did not take control of a hooked fish early enough. Responsibility is therefore the key word when presenting heavy bolt rigs.

# How to enjoy Irish Pike on the fly

Now, this is no blarney. Irish pike caught on the fly rod from beautiful, 125-acre Castle Hume Lough – which is connected to the lower Lough Erne system near Enniskillen, Northern Ireland, and overlooked by the Lough Erne Golf Resort (anyone staying at the resort can fish Castle Hume) – provided boat partner John Horsey and myself with some memorable battles.

Being England's most capped fly-fishing international and a totally professional fly-fishing guide, who operates out of Chew Valley Lake, John, from Somerset, was the perfect boat partner in what turned out to be very difficult fishing conditions because of an extremely chilly north-easterly wind. But by systematically working various depth bands (the lake varied between three and 20-feet deep, with a huge area shelving down to 30 feet in the centre) – and by continually double haul casting on the drift, punching out virtually a full fly line every cast to present our flies as far away from the boat as possible – we started to score. This was due, in no small part, to the large, effective pike flies John ties using flash material that provides great shine and bulk, but which is light to cast.

We had each taken four, 9 weight outfits along, our 10-foot rods and selections of floating to extremely fast sinking lines geared to cover all expected situations. And with most fish keeping close to the bottom (the water temperature was very low), medium and fast sinking lines proved best by far. From around the margins, well covered in reed and sedges, where depth varied between three and six feet, we attracted jacks only to around 7lbs. But when we concentrated our drifts over depths between eight and 15 feet, the bigger fish started to show; beautifully marked and spotted pike, in the 10-16lbs bracket, that went deep and stayed there for several minutes in unbelievably powerful fights.

Mostly, they wanted that fly stripped in fast. Had I lost my first fish, which weighed 14lbs, I would have sworn it was 10lbs larger, such was the account it gave. They were definitely not hitting our flies with much aggression. And we missed numerous half-hearted pulls, when they only nipped at the fly's tail; something we attributed to the cold wind and exceedingly clear water conditions. But we were more than pleased with several propeller-tailed, stunningly spotted pike to 16lbs, such as the beauty John and I are displaying here.

4

# Ingredients for SUCCESS

• Natural • Manufactured and Lures • Groundbaiting

"Success is simple. Do what's right, the right way, at the right time."

Freshwater Baits

# Natural

## Understanding aquatic flies 442

If you were left high and dry, miles from nowhere at a river or lakeland fishery having forgotten the bait, what would you honestly do? Well, if rummaging about turning over logs in search of worms fails to produce, and their isn't a grocer's shop for miles, being able to identify the life cycle of some of our more common aquatic flies would help enormously. Especially that of the sedge fly whose larva are called caddis grubs.

## Hunting down caddis grubs 443

To collect these grubs, a foray amongst the shallows, turning over large pieces of flint and sunken logs to which caddis cling in their homemade cases, is the way to obtain a batch for bait. And as the average-sized caddis grub is twice that of a shop-bought maggot, most cyprinid species can be subsequently targeted.

## Preparing caddis grubs 444

To use caddis, each, creamy-coloured, succulent grub has to be carefully removed (using the finger nails of thumb and forefinger) from its protective and intricate case manufactured from twigs and sand particles, while squeezing gently at the opposite end. And hey presto, out it comes. Hook gently through the head with a size 14 hook. After an hour's rummaging about enjoying the rewards of bait collecting, you will have collected enough caddis grubs for a morning's long-trotting, or lift-float fishing for tench or carp. Give them a try.

## Lobworms: successful snitching

If you fancy owning a supply of lobworms on demand for occasions when the
ground is frozen solid, or the local tackle shop has run out, why not try gath
your own. The secret for successful snitching is collecting worms from the la
night during a mild evening following a good down pour. Then you'll find ma
the worms almost completely out of their holes. Those barely out, which requ
mini tug of war often break and so cannot be kept less they contaminate the
Remember to creep stealthily and use a wide-beam torch that isn't too harsh
Extreme light and heavy vibrations make worms retreat quickly into their hol
your garden does not produce or you live in a flat, then simply pop along to
local cricket pitch where for much of the year the grass is kept short. Hang a
gallon plastic bucket on a cord around your neck which keeps both hands en
free: one for the torch, the other for picking up worms. Walk slowly and care
picking up your feet just like a chicken does, and you will never worry about
supply of lobworms again.

## Storing lobworms

446

To store lobworms for future trips (lobs last best in temperatures between 35 and 45 degrees F), it's worth all the trouble of constructing a box made from ½ inch plywood. It should be at least 20 inches square and have two lids - top and bottom - with a dozen or so one eighth of an inch diameter holes drilled through each of the sides. The best medium, in which lobs will live quite happily and remain in good condition for at least several months, is dampened, shredded newspaper. Simply tear old newspapers into one to two inch strips and soak the lot in the sink. Wring the paper out well and place in your worm box together with your supply of lobworms. Remember to turn the box upside down every couple of weeks (hence the need for two lids) so the inhabitants keep working through the paper.

## Worm conditioning

447

The term worm conditioning may seem a trifle up market, but try it for yourself using lobworms, which are popped just a dozen or so at a time into a two pint plastic bait box, along with some soaking wet shredded newspaper. Tear the newspaper into one inch strips before soaking and wringing out most (but not all) of the water. Then simply leave in a fridge for at least several weeks. After only one week, however, your worms will have turned into veritable snakes, fatter, stronger and more lively than you have ever fished with before.

## ing cockles

448

kles may be a sea bait, but when purchased in bulk ready lled and boiled from the fishmonger, they can easily be split up separate batches and even coloured before bagging up and ping straight into the freezer. Use a teaspoon of carp bait dye a pint or two of cockles and swish around in a bait box together n a cupful of boiling water, and strain off the excess colour. ality roach and rudd in addition to tench, bream, chub, barbel d carp etc, all love this bait, which can be presented float fished ledgered singly on the hook or hair-rigged 2-5 up.

## se an aquarium net

449

procure all manner of natural baits, try holding a small square-aped fine mesh aquarium net vertically hard against the bottom a brook or stream, immediately behind a large piece of flint, fore lifting it up. Small fish like stone loach, bullheads and even ook lampreys, all much loved by chub, barbel and perch, often oot straight downstream into the net. So keep a small net in the oot of your car, should you ever be stuck for bait.

## axworms

450

ecialist pet shops stock all manner of natural baits ch cyprinid species love. Mealworms for instance which much, much longer than unrefrigerated maggots, are ilable in four sizes from minis to super giants. And how out waxworms, larvae of the waxmoth. This juicy, buoyant, amy-white grub is a prime trotting bait for roach, dace, ub and grayling, if carefully hooked through the tail. axworms keep for long periods in the tub in which they me packed, if kept at a temperature of between 55-60 grees F. Even larger still are tebos, larvae of a moth ported from Chile, which feeds beneath the bark of a Tebos ee, hence its name. Best kept at a temperature of between 5-50 degrees F, they are larger than a wasp grub and ll attract all cyprinids from specimen-sized dace to carp. esent on a size 12 hook or two up on a size 10.

## Freshwater Baits

# Natural

### Making dead baits more attractive 451

As far as predators like pike and zander are concerned, dead baits are not just dead baits. They can be flavoured (by injecting with various fish oils) and even 'coloured', which really gives them great appeal. Simply put some powdered bait dye into a clean bait box and mix with a little water. Then, gripping by the tail with forceps swish each 'thawed' dead bait about till even in colour, and leave for a while on newspaper for the excess liquid to blot off before re-freezing or using straight away. Alternatively, simply paint on liquid food dye (available from the grocers in amazing colours) with a small brush, straight from the bottle. Pale coloured fish such as sprats, smelt and herrings look amazing in yellow or gold, while any fish coloured in red simply oozes 'colour appeal'. But the choice is yours and the permutations are limited only by your imagination

### Locusts, house crickets and grasshoppers 4

If you love close range dapping for crafty, clear-water chub from amongst the cover of marginal grasses, then locusts, house crick and grasshoppers are summer baits you just cannot ignore. Whet you present them downstream on the surface in conjunction with small floating controller like the tenpin and a greased line, or sim dangle or dap directly beneath the rod tip into gaps in the surfac weed, these highly attractive baits available from any specialist pet will catch you chub when others won't. They can be easily kept in a old aquarium (preferably in the kitchen in 75-80 degrees F) with piece of tightly fitting gauze on top, and advice on feeding them w freely given from the pet shop where you bought them.

### Presenting dead static baits 453

Using big baits for pike, whether live or dead, does not guarantee catching larger specimens, as a jack will grab at a live bait of at least half its own size, while a 20lbs specimen will suck up a sprat from the bottom. In fact, presentation is perhaps more important, in that dead baits presented static on the bottom where they are easily hoovered up by larger pike does produce pike of a higher average size than, say, working small spinners or live baits.

### Bloodworms 45

Blood worms are so devastatingly effective because they are in most waters the staple, natural food of all cyprinid species from a three inc rudd, all the way up to a 40lbs carp. But due to their minute size, th can really only be presented on tiny hooks (sizes 22-26) and light lines. So while most big cyprinids tench and carp in particular, actuall grow to huge proportions by gorging daily upon vast quantities of bloodworms, they are in no way considered a big-fish bait. The delica style of pole fishing is tailor made for presenting these little red men which are the larva of the midge fly. And in British freshwaters there are close on 400 different species of midges, which is why they are such a major food item. Plumbing the depth of your swim accurately imperative because the ideal way of presenting bloodworms is just off bottom. Feed in joker (tiny midge larva) either neat or in damp loam a pole cup to draw in the fish and present your bloodworm over the

## ...w your worms 455

...s are not just worms. Each of the four popular fishing worms found in ...h soil has its own very special uses. The smallest, found in heaps of rotting ..., is the humble redworm. These short, slow-moving worms are much loved ...ch, bream, roach, dace and grayling, and because they do not wriggle off the ... are great with barb-less hooks and for baiting the hooks on spinners for ...d attraction. Slightly larger is the brandling, which is found in manure heaps. ...ly, gyrating worm easily recognisable by the yellowy-orange rings around its ...nd by the pungent yellow fluid that seeps out as you hook it, the brandling ...asily wriggle off the hook if a maggot or caster is not nicked on afterwards. ...natively, nick onto the point of the hook and over the barb, a small section of ... of an inch diameter elastic band. Twice the size of a brandling, and therefore ...able mouthful for cyprinid species of all sizes, plus perch, catfish and eels, is ...endrobaena, a chunky 3-4 inch red worm that was originally imported from ...nd, but which is now commonly bred in this country. Lastly, but by no means ... because it is in all probability the most versatile, effective worm of all, comes ...obworm and I cannot possibly think of a British freshwater species that won't ...le one up. See Tips 445, 446 and 447.

## Using freshly killed maggots 456

When feeder fishing in silty-bottomed lakes for summer tench and bream and filling an open end feeder with maggots, sandwiched between a plug of dampened bread crumbs at each end, be aware that within seconds of your feeder touching bottom those maggots will bury into the silt and be lost from sight. The remedy here is to use only freshly killed maggots in the feeder (which don't crawl away and get lost) by either blanching them in hot water, or placing them in a polythene bag and squeezing out all the air before tying the bag up tightly and placing it in the freezer for at least 24 hours. Job sorted!

## Elderberries 457

Elderberries are truly one of the great natural trotting baits for species like dace, roach chub and even barbel, especially when loose feeding with stewed hempseed or tares. Being larger than hempseed they generally sort out a better stamp of roach and dace too. Collect elderberries in the autumn before they become over-ripe and store them in a large (wide-necked) preserving jar containing glycerine or a solution of dilute formalin. Do not pull them directly off the bush or they will squash. Cut off little bunches containing around 20-30 berries and pop straight into the jar. When required, and elderberries are great throughout both summer and winter months. Simply give them a good rinse in cold water before use.

## Keeping baits cool 458

To keep maggots or casters cool during a long drive, simply pop a frozen freezer pack or two into your bait bucket.

## Avoid losing bait 459

To stop free-lined or float-fished, lip-hooked live baits or dead baits flying off on a lengthy cast, simply sleeve a ¼ inch section of ¼ inch wide elastic band onto the hook after the bait. Remember to work the hook gently outwards from the top lip so the point is free. You will connect with far more perch or chub in this way because the hook point will be angled in the correct position for striking when the bait is engulfed in the predator's jaws.

## Switch to sweetcorn 460

Whenever minnows become a nuisance and get to your trotted maggots before roach or dace, simply switch over to casters or sweetcorn.

## Dead minnows as feed 461

Minnows, dead ones that is, make a great scatter loose feed when targeting eels, zander, or monster chub during the hours of darkness. If you forget to catch a supply and freeze down for later use, pop into your local delicatessen or super market and buy a frozen batch of 'whitebait', which is really a tiny sardine. A handful can then be scattered into a few likely, pre-selected swims every other day say for a week, prior to your first session.

# Manufactured Baits and Lures

## Presenting pellets

462

Here is a quick and easy way of presenting any trout, carp or other pellet as hook bait, without softening, or threading onto a hair rig. It works with boilies too. Using super-glue, glue a pellet onto a strip of 1/8th of an inch wide elastic band, and trim close leaving enough of a tab at one end to put your hook through. For presenting two-up, either glue two side by side onto the band, or glue the second onto the end of the first. Easy peasy. You can even vary where the pellet sits on the hook by easing the band around the bend, so it hangs immediately below, or ease it around to midway along the shank so it is presented similar to a hair rig.

## Commercial bait bands

463

Commercially produced bait bands (mini silicon bands), which stretch completely around the pellet, also work well with all pellet sizes between 5 and 12mm. The pellets can simply be pushed into the bait band and positioned on the back of the hook shank in a prime position to ensure a good hook hold. Larger pellets are best drilled and hair-rigged.

## Wobbling spoons

464

When casting spoons for pike, zander and even salmon, maintain their fluttering action whatever the depth, by carrying a selection of the same lure in various weights from ¼ up to an ounce. Then you can wobble large, but light spoons over even shallow, weedy water for pike, or clip on a heavy model (of the same size) for counting-down (at around one foot per second) when working it just a couple of feet above bottom.

## Presenting cheese and meat

4

All manner of soft cheese and meat cubes such as luncheon meat or ham (don't forget turkey, chicken, chipolatas etc) can be effectively presented simply by pushing the hook through the cen of the cube (cut your cubes roughly to the length of the hook's shank so it can be pulled through) and rotating it so that the be and point bed into a corner and disappear out of sight once the is gently pulled. It is far better, however, to use a one inch hair so that the bait is presented off the hook. For instant penetratio it is without question the ultimate confidence setup, when you ar bolt-rig or standard ledgering.

## ticky pellets 466

/hen preparing hard pellet feed for moulding around a
nethod feeder so they do not break up during the cast, try
ot to over wet them. Alternatively, make them really sticky
y adding the juice from a tin of sweetcorn. This not only
softens the pellets, but adds that sweet aroma much loved
by bream, carp and tench. Once added, stir regularly for 15
minutes until, when squeezed, a ball of pellets sticks together.
Adding the corn is yet another option.

## Rubbery cheese as second baits 468

Cheese chunks, particularly those broken from a block of rubbery-type cheese, like Maasdan, Edam or Gouda from Holland, Jarlsberg from Norway, or Subenhard and Danbo from Denmark (explore your local cheese shop) all make fine second baits to luncheon meat when rolling meat for barbel and chub. They really stay on the hook well.

## Shiny spoons 469

In addition to that irresistible wobbling action, their flash is what attracts predators to spoons. So don't fish firing on only half your cylinders by using tarnished and dull metal lures. Restore to their ultimate brilliance and attraction by using a strong paste-type, or metal polish cleaner and buff up so each reflects the maximum amount of light. And whilst you're at it, replace any bent or rusted treble hooks and split rings. Specially-designed split-ring pliers will stop your finger and thumb nails from splitting, and complete the job in seconds.

## king cheese paste 467

oftest, most pliable cheese paste which chub, barbel, carp and
all adore is easily made from old bread (crust removed) and
k of Cheddar. Soak the bread, and it must be old, in water
vring out well, mashing it between your fingers into a creamy
. Then grate the cheese finely and take time kneading it into
read paste. A mix of around two parts bread to one part
e makes a super paste. For a stronger colour, knead in a little
e powdered carp bait dye or use Red Leicester in stead of
lar. And for added aromatic attraction (especially for chub)
de a good helping of grated parmesan cheese over the paste
nead well in.

## Synthetic rubber shads 470

When looking for an artificial lure that will cast like a bullet, is heavy enough to be counted down to the bottom of deep water where rocks and snags could pose problems, and one that will work with equal effectiveness for pike in reservoirs and Scottish lochs to the monster Nile perch of Egypt's Lake Nasser, then synthetic rubber shads have no equal. And because most internal lead-heads like Storm's wild-eye swim shads come rigged with just a large single (upward-pointing) hook, as opposed to duos of trebles, they snag up far less than most artificials.

Freshwater Baits

# Manufactured Baits and Lures

## 471 Making designer paste

Making your own designer paste allows you to create unique bait that no one else is using (particularly on hard-fished waters) giving you a distinct edge. In a liquidiser, you can pulverise any kind of trout, halibut or carp pellet for instance and reduce it to a fine powder to which raw eggs are added (as a binding agent) before kneading into a ball of pliable paste. All the feed-pellets sold at aquarium and garden centres for koi carp work well, as do such products like pig pellets, rabbit pellets, even chicken pellets. The only addition (apart from raw eggs) that you might like to try is sprinkling a tablespoon of Phillips Yeast Mixture (a powder available from cage bird shops) over the paste and kneading in. It has a strong, pungent aroma much loved by carp especially. The ingredients used for making your own boilies also make great pastes simply by kneading in enough eggs. Those with milk derivatives in the base mix, and especially bird food mixes, also work well to which colouring (in the form of powder dye) can also be added. Add a teaspoon of flavouring to a little water and knead into the mix if you so wish. The permutations for paste making are simply endless. It's good (if somewhat messy at times) fun too.

## 472 Colouring sweetcorn

Colouring sweetcorn could give you an edge over other anglers and educated fish. Start by pouring off all the liquid (great for adding to ground bait or for sticking pellet feed together when method-feeder fishing) and empty the contents of a tin into a poly bag. Add your chosen colour (SuperCook liquid colourings are great for this) you'll only need a few drops because it is highly concentrated, and then twist the bag to seal it. Now give the bag a good shake, and hey presto your corn is coloured. Use immediately, or freeze for later sessions. Incidentally, if you use a lot of sweetcorn, buying large bags of frozen corn from supermarkets gives you twice as much for your money as opposed to purchasing in tins. A point well worth remembering. Also worth remembering is that corn is one of the finest baits to use as a cocktail, with maggots, a red worm, a meal worm, casters, a small cube of bread crust etc.

## 473 Pop-up style

For presenting pop-up style over dense bottom weed, your corn can be sleeved onto a hair rig. Thread a real grain onto the hair first, followed by a buoyant kernel of imitation corn. You can even colour this too. If using a long hook length, add an AA shot between 3-10 inches (depending upon weed height) above the bait, thus counterbalancing the buoyancy of the bait. If small species become a nuisance by pecking your corn to bits, use cooked maize instead which is larger and harder. See ground baiting Tip 482. It too can be coloured in the same way. But you'll need two kernels of imitation corn to pop up one of maize.

## Soak seeds

The old way of preparing a batch of hard particles hempseed (before we knew better) was to boil and simmer the seeds in an old saucepan on the cooke 30 minutes or so, and completely stink the kitchen The modern way is to first soak the seeds for a co of days in cold water (and this applies incidentally preparation of most particles except for tiger nuts maize) before straining off the water and putting th seeds into a plastic bucket with a rip-off lid, and th covering with boiling water to a depth of two inches Press the lid on firmly and allow the seeds to stew swell in their own juices for a minimum of 24 hour during which time they will split (showing that tiny w shoot) and darken almost to black.

## 47 Extra power

Leaving stewed hempseed for two or three days in the bucket almost until it starts fermenting creates extra pulling power to some species, carp ir particular. Or the freshly stewed seeds (always do a sizeable batch) can be split into session-sized portions and popped into the freezer for later use.

# arge or small, an easy neal is all a pike wants

ring the 25 years I ran a tackle shop in the middle Norwich, many a young angler came in for advice on w to catch big pike from the Norfolk Broads. And my vice today would be exactly the same as it was then. eeline, ledger or float-ledger an aromatic sea dead it (herring, smelt or mackerel) on the bottom, perfectly atic'. Because the big old girls [as all pike of 15lbs plus ;, males rarely exceeding double figures] like to suck meals that do not attempt to get away. Being, for the st part, much more sedentary compared to 'jacks', pike want their meals on the table, just like elderly ople. They don't want to chase after hamburgers and on the run like teenagers.

advice was once taken too far by one young customer, o, having purchased a couple of mackerel from local fishmonger to follow my 'static' deadbaiting hnique, accounted for a fine 24lbs pike from Ormesby oads. When he excitedly related the story of its capture d mentioned he had to 'throw' each bait out by hand cause they were impossible to cast, I asked exactly w big they were. " Oh, around 2lbs apiece" came the ly. I was flabbergasted to say the least. But then pike unpredictable and my young customer was indeed tunate to 'hook up' positively using such massive bait.

It is equally true that pike will have a go at almost anything on occasion. Using a three-inch diving plug along the margins of a deep gravel pit, for instance, I once caught an 18lbs pike that, only minutes before, had swallowed a young coot. How do I know? Well, I saw the unfortunate bird disappear beneath the surface in a huge swirl [which prompted my casting over the spot] and, upon retrieval of my lure, it coughed up a wodge of sodden feathers. The event proved to me, beyond doubt, that there is, of course, no 'best bait size' for pike. Given the chance, they will attack virtually anything that looks like an easy meal.

While playing what turned out to be my largest ever roach/rudd hybrid several years back, hooked on light float tackle in a weedy lake, it was suddenly grabbed – and, fortunately, released after a few seconds – by a pike that looked to be no more than about eight pounds. And, yet, that huge hybrid tipped the scales at only an ounce below 4lbs – roughly half the size of the pike.

## JOHN'S TOP PIKE BAIT TIP

The old adage of using big bait if you want big pike does not necessarily add up. In many cases, the problems of hooking up are greater with larger baits. Which is why, whether live or deadbaiting, I prefer whole fish or half baits in the five- to 8-inch size bracket. I can then wind down and strike instantly in one progressive action, knowing I have more than a fair chance of the hooks finding purchase.

# Manufactured Baits and Lures

## Go static

476

If you have trouble with dead baits flying off your hooks during the cast and even on the retrieve when targeting pike and zander, remember that when presenting the bait static it's best to first firmly work the barbed point of the top treble on your wire trace (semi barb-less trebles are kinder to both predator and angler) into the sinewy tail root. The muscles here make for a perfect hold. The second treble (barbed prong only) can then be inserted 2-3 inches down the flank. For wobbling dead baits which obviously appear more natural if swimming head first (wish I had a fiver for every pike that has grabbed hold of a static bait being retrieved tail-first) simply reverse the order by working two prongs of the top treble into the baits eye socket, and the barbed prong of the lower treble firmly into the flank. Get used to inspecting the bait following each retrieve and readjust the hooks accordingly when they appear to have worked loose.

## Eel heads

478

Catching eels during the warmer months on worm or maggot baits intended for other species can become a nuisance. But why not turn such occasions to your advantage, assuming you go fishing for pike and zander during the winter, by taking those eels home (12-18 inch fish are ideal) and freezing down for later use. The head end of an eel especially, due to the amount of blood it contains, and the fact that it casts like a bullet, is one incredibly effective dead bait. Along with the lamprey, eels are in fact my top bait for pike when fishing the Norfolk Broads and their connecting tidal rivers. And I invariably stop the car whenever I am driving beside a fenland drain and see a dredger heaping great piles of silt up along the bank. Wriggling from the silt could be enough eels to last me all winter.

## Use a cable a tie

If you experience soft pastes coming off the hook whilst pole fish simply wrap a small plastic cable-tie around the pole (and cut o the tag end to leave an inch or so protruding) several inches ab where your hook lies when the rig is laid alongside the pole top. Then you simply hang your baited hook over the tag whilst ship the pole out without the paste touching the surface.

## Jumbo peanuts

I am classifying peanuts as manufactured bait because they do aft all, like sweetcorn, have to be planted and grown. And when you c obtain some of the American jumbo-sized peanuts, there are few effective particle baits for both tench and carp, used either float fi with the lift-method or on a bolt-rig ledger set-up. Try it side-h or presented two, or even three-up on a hair. I've enjoyed no sma amount of success with chub and barbel whilst ledgering with pea too. Part of their success is that being hard they deter small nuisa species, and being decidedly buoyant makes them perfect for pres over or amongst weed beds. To really pop them up, however, cut a of rig foam to the shape and size of a peanut and place it last on hair so it floats the others off the bottom.

## Preparing peanuts

Ready-shelled (un-roasted) standard-sized peanuts are perfec loose feeding, but both these and the jumbo hook baits do need properly prepared by first soaking for 24 hours in cold water. St off and having put them in a plastic tub with a rip-off lid, cover to a depth of several inches with boiling water. Put the lid firmly and leave for 48 hours, after which they will have swollen to twice their size and be ready, after straining off all the excess liquid, fo immediate use or bagging up in session-sized batches for poppi into the freezer. You can even colour them. See Tip 472.

## Hooking stewed seeds

If you find difficulty putting stewed hempseed onto the hook, here's to do it. Find a seed that has only just split open (a little of its white seed protruding) and gently grip between thumb and forefinger to f the split open further, whilst inserting the bend of a fine wire size 14 hook. Wide gape, spade-end hooks are perfect for presenting hemps

Freshwater Baits

# Ground Baiting

## Maize

482

Maize takes some beating, both as a hook bait and ground bait for just about every cyprinid species, from the heaviest carp to quality-sized roach. This is even more important these days, particularly with aggressively marketed designer baits, which by comparison are vastly more expensive. A 25kg sack of whole or plate maize will set you back less than one large pack of boilies. But because it is hard, it does require careful preparation.

## Preparing maize

483

To prepare hard maize, start by soaking the grains in water for a few days. They eventually swell into super, yellowy-orange kernels with a distinct, nutty, wheaty, pop-corn aroma. Then either pressure cook for 20 minutes, or prepare in the microwave (albeit in small batches) in a shallow bowl of water. The finished (now-split) kernels, three times the size of the original, can be hooked on one, two or three up or sleeved onto a hair rig. Cooked maize also forms the base of varying ground baits. It can be added to a breadcrumb-based ground bait for bream or tench fishing (really sinks quickly in deep, fast flowing rivers) or added to seeds and pulses to form a wonderful particle mix. Buy a sack and experiment. See Manufactured baits Tip 474.

## Liquidised bread in cold conditions

Liquidised bread is a fabulous loose feed when using punched-bread or small pieces of crust or flake on the hook for species like dace, roach an chub. To prepare a batch, remove the crusts from several slices of fresh white bread, and after tearing into pieces, put them all into a food liquidi and pulse. Literally in a few seconds the bread is reduced by the machin blades into thousands of tiny, moist particles. When squeezed gently tog these can be thrown underarm into the head of the swim, where they slo descend and break up into a cascade-like snow-storm of a cloud. So overfeeding the shoal is never a problem with this loose feed. This is wh works so beautifully in cold conditions.

## Heavy ground bait

If you want a really heavy ground bait for attracting bream living in fast rivers, which gets down there fast whatever the depth, start with base of well-wetted coarse bread crumbs (shop bought). Alternativel make up a batch of mashed bread by soaking old bread in water for 20 minutes and then mashing it between your fingers whilst squeezi most of the excess water out. Add several cupfuls of flaked maize an the same of pearl barley, which really stiffen up the mix. To improve i further, add a cupful of what you intend using as hook baits, such as chopped worms, stewed wheat, maize, sweetcorn, casters or maggots so on. Finally, knead well into hard cricket balls for throwing out.

## ‸ tape 486

nd baiting distant swims for species like
el and chub in fast-flowing rivers can be
ved in two ways. You can repeatedly use
od (see Tip 491) or a large swim feeder to
sit a bed of bait on the riverbed prior to
ng. Or, invest in some PVA tape. You can
, using a long stringer baiting needle, thread
up to a dozen or so boilies, cubes of meat,
ce or drilled pellets etc, and push them all
the needle onto a length of tape and nick the
nt of your hook (already baited up hair-rig
e) into one end. Within minutes of casting out,
tape will dissolve leaving a scattering of loose
d right next to your hook bait. See diagram.

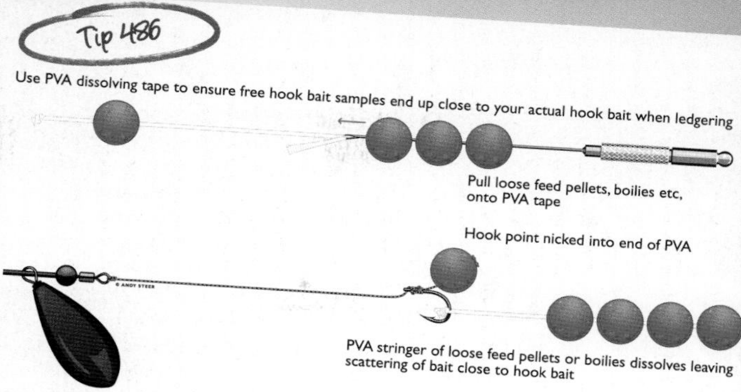


## und baiting for pike 487

nd baiting for predators like pike, can work wonders.
se a still water (not too far from home) where pike exist
od numbers and select a commanding position from
to introduce free offerings every day for a week or so,
as a long, deep gully between islands, or a promontory
ng into deep water. Those cert-looking swims covering
areas are what to look for.

## -baiting 488

ase fish in bulk for pre-baiting and cut each into
sections (head-middle and tail-end) before freezing
into packs of a dozen or so pieces (your daily baiting
of fish pieces). Or perhaps you already have a freezer
old baits just waiting to be experimented with. Either
fter a week or so of pre-baiting, try a session and
some hectic action. This routine also works well on
rivers particularly at confluences where dykes, drains
other rivers join the main flow. Always great pike and
er movement areas these, that are simply crying out for
baiting attention.

## Ground-baiting whilst fishing 489

For ground baiting whilst fishing, there is nothing to beat the addition of a PVA stick made from mesh, or a clear bag filled with hook bait samples or complementary pellet feed, nicked onto your hook prior to casting out. Because when this synthetic material dissolves within seconds of your bait settling on the lake or river bed, an attractive carpet of loose feed (your ground bait really) is spread around it. Remember to add only oils to your loose feed, or you'll melt the mesh or bag before casting. See also Tip 485.

## Keep floating casters 490

Don't throw away those old floating casters. Store in a poly bag in the freezer and when you have at least a couple of pints or three, thaw out and utilise by crushing in your hands over a tub of coarse brown bread crumbs, so all the attractive juices are squeezed out to dampen the crumbs. The myriad of broken brown shells give the ground bait a lovely flecked appearance, and if you add hook bait fragments like fresh casters maggots or corn as filling for an open-end feeder, there is little to beat it for bream and tench. You can add the juice from the tin of sweetcorn too.

## Ground baiting with a spod 491

The best way to ground bait a distant swim for carp, tench and bream, if you do not have access to a boat, is with a spod. These high-density plastic, rocket-like projectiles can be loaded with all kinds of particles, mini boilies or pellet feed and they will cast to exactly where you wish to place them. But you do need a long, powerful rod (not your fishing rod - something heavier) and strong reel line to cope with the repeated casting and retrieving. Three-quarter fill the spod with bait and cast to the desired spot. Then, before retrieving, pass the line around the line clip on your spool so that each successive cast lands in more or less the same spot, provided you overhead cast straight out.

## Avoid spills 492

Remember to only fill the spod to the three-quarter mark. All the bait will then stay in the spod during the cast, with no spills or wastage. There are no prizes for scattering bait all over the lake.

## Clipping your outfit 493

To ensure your baited rig ends up in the same spot as your spodded bait, clip up your fishing outfit or outfits, to exactly the same distance as on the spod rod, by walking the rigs out along the bank with the reel's bale arm open. It's worth the effort.

Freshwater Baits

# Ground Baiting

## Catapulting ground bait

494

Catapulting out ground bait is probably the most commonly used method of pre-baiting and feeding up swims beyond throwing range. And provided you follow a few simple rules, distances of up to 50 yards can be achieved. Purchase a proper ground bait catapult fitted with a large, rigid pouch or a plastic mesh-type pouch (which stops the ball from disintegrating when you pull back the elastic) and strong, durable elastic.

## Keep catapult bait balls small

495

The secret of catapulting out ground bait is not making the balls of bait too large. Slightly bigger than a golf ball is absolute tops. Otherwise you will achieve neither distance or any degree of accuracy. And do not add loose feed such as maggots to the mix, which will split the ball apart when they start to wriggle. Dead maggots are fine.

## Boiled rice

496

Boiled rice makes a fine base for light ground baits to which small particles such as mung beans, buck wheat, red dari seeds, stewed wheat and sweet corn may be added. To colour rice yellow, simply add a spoonful of turmeric to the boiling water.

## Stewed wheat

497

One of the cheapest and most effective bulk ground bait additives is stewed wheat. You can buy an entire sack for just a few quid, and it's so easy to prepare, both to use as hook bait and for stiffening a crumb-based ground bait.

## Colouring stewed wheat

To prepare stewed wheat in bulk, follow the directions for hempseed in manufactured baits Tip 474. To colour stewed wheat, simply add a spoonf or two of powdered carp bait dye (the colour of your choice) when coveri the particles in boiling water in a plastic tub with a rip-off lid. Stir thoro before pressing the lid on and leaving for a minimum of 24 hours. Then off any surplus liquid and your bait is ready.

## Preparing small batches of wheat

Here's a great tip for preparing just a small batch of wheat to use as hoo baits or for mixing in with ground bait on the evening before the mornin you go fishing, should you have forgotten to arrange fresh bait. Pour a c or two of wheat into a vacuum flask and top up with boiling water. Not ri to the top or when the wheat expands, the flask could explode. About thr quarters full is about right, before screwing the cap on. In the morning, empty the contents into a bait tin, now perfectly stewed and nicely swollen showing the white grain inside, and smelling distinctly nutty, and you're ready to go.

## Black-eyed beans

Black-eyed beans are super particle bait, which can be easily prepared a coloured for adding to your ground bait mix (follow the directions given Tip 474 of Manufactured Baits and Lures). Black eyes can be hair rigge side hooked and either float fished or ledgered bolt-rig style.

## Tick beans

Tick beans are a large, shiny dark-brown particle that carp and tench bo irresistible when prepared as for stewed wheat (Tip 498) and the bait is t impervious to the attentions of small, nuisance species. They are therefor perfect ground bait additive. Present two-up on a hair and size 8 hook w loose feeding with tares and hempseed for barbel. They are deadly.